Texas Notary Journal
for
Notary Signing Agents

by
Brian Greul

Introduction

Thank you for purchasing the Texas Notary Journal for Notary Signing Agents. This book has been designed to meet the needs of Texas Notary Signing Agents. It is intended to facilitate efficient, accurate, and detailed notary records, as required by Texas Government Code.

This book is designed to facilitate the typical loan closing with 1 or 2 signers. To assist in making detailed records, each document notarized should be recorded on one line. The fee may be recorded, along with the notarization type(s) and the date of the document. Each signer who the document was notarized for should initial that line. The most common closing documents are pre-printed for convenience. Please see more detailed instructions on pages X and Y.

Should you have suggestions or feedback on ways to improve this book please send email to Books@OcotilloPress.com

©2019,2020 Ocotillo Press
ISBN 978-1-954285-00-2

Printed in the United States of America
Fourth Printing, 2020

Ocotillo Press
5103 Laurel Creek Way
Houston, TX 77017
Books@OcotilloPress.com

Disclaimer: As a Notary Public you are responsible for ensuring that your practice is proper and in compliance. Every attempt has been made to ensure that this record book complies with the requirements of the State of Texas. Nonetheless, the author and publisher disclaim any liability for the content or use of this record book.

Notary Signing Agent (NSA) is a registered trademark of the National Notary Association (NNA) and NNA Services LLC. The NNA is not a sponsor or affiliate of the publisher of this record book and is not a contributor of the content.
For more information on becoming an NSA visit http://nationalnotary.org

This record book belongs to:

Notary Name:	
Notary Address:	
Notary City, State, Zip:	
Notary Residence County:	
Notary Phone:	
Notary Phone:	
Notary Email:	

Record Book Dates of Use:

Date of First Use	Date of Last Use

Notary Commission Information:

State	Commission Number	Commission Expiration

Official Signature:

x_____

Emergency Contact Information:

Emergency Contact 1	Emergency Contact 2

In the event of the death or incapacitation of the Notary this book shall be turned in to the County Clerk Office in the County where the Notary Resides. The Notary's seal shall be destroyed to prevent misuse.

The Texas Secretary of State advises that the Notary shall maintain this journal in a safe place for the longer of the term in which the notarization occurred or 3 years following the date of the notarization. Best practice, however, would be for the notary to permanently maintain copies of the records. (Source: Texas Secretary of State Website)

The NNA recommends a 10 year retention period.

Signer 1 Name and Address: (A)			Signer and A
(B)			
Identification (C) nod: ☐ Personally Known ☐ Other ☐ Texas Driver's License ☐ Driver's License ☐ Passport			Identi ☐ Tex
(D)			
(E) Sign Here			
X _____		X _	
Date/Time: (F)		(G) Ref#	
Signing Address: (H)			
Document Date	Notarization	Document Description	

A)Name of the Signer

B)Official or claimed address of the signer

C) Checkbox for the type of ID used. If Other note in area D. Credible witness goes in D.

D)expiration date or other data related to ID.

NOTE: Do not record the ID Number or biometric data.

E) Signature (not required in Texas)

F) Date and Time of the Notarization

G) Reference Number

H) Address where Notarization took place if different from official address of signer.

Document Date	Notarization Ack Jur Oth Fee if any	Document Description		Signer Initials	
				1	2
(J)	(K) (I)	Deed of Trust / tgage (L)		(M) (N)	
		Deed - Genera it Claim - Special Warranty			
		Borrower's Title Affidavit			

I) Fee, if charged for notarizing this document. Note Texas sets limits on what can be charged for notary services.

J) The date on the document being notarized

K) The type of notarization performed. Acknowledgement, Jurat, Other.

L) The type of document being notarized. Use a blank line to record a document type not listed here. Line through what does not apply.

M/N) After notarization each signer should initial to indicate that the document was notarized.

		(R)			
$					

Notes: (P)

Ack:Do you a ledge this as your signature and your free act and deed, for the purposes stated herein?
Jurat: Do you (Q) nly (swear/affirm) that this statement is true, (so help you God / on your honor)?

P) This area is for recording any notes or comments that relate to the notarization or signing. Deed related information can be recorded here as well to comply with Texas requirements.

Q) Read these aloud for each notarization performed.

R) Blank lines for document types not listed on form.

Signer 1 Name and Address:		Signer 2 Name and Address:	

Signer 1 Identification Method: ☐ Personally Known ☐ Other
☐ Texas Driver's License ☐ Driver's License ☐ Passport

Signer 2 Identification Method: ☐ Personally Known ☐ Other
☐ Texas Driver's License ☐ Driver's License ☐ Passport

Sign Here
X _____

Sign Here
X _____

Date/Time: **Ref#:**

Signing Address:

Document Date	Notarization **Ack Jur Oth** Fee if any	Document Description	Signer Initials 1	2
		Deed of Trust / Mortgage		
		Deed - General - Quit Claim - Special Warranty		
		Borrower's Title Affidavit		
		Borrower's Closing Affidavit		
		E&O / Compliance Agreement		
		Occupancy Affidavit		
		Signature Name Affidavit		
		Power of Attorney - Limited / Durable		
		T-47 Residential Real Property Affidavit		
		Mineral Rights Acknowledgement and Agreement		
		Designation of Homestead / Non-Homestead		
		Notice of Penalties for Making False or Misleading Statements		
		Ownership Affidavit		
		Occupancy and Financial Status Affidavit		
		Obligation of Debts Affidavit		
		Release of Claims and Hold Harmless Agreement		
		Affidavit of Marital Status		
		Tax Indemnity		
		Compliance / Correction Agreement		

Notes:

Ack:Do you acknowledge this as your signature and your free act and deed, for the purposes stated herein?
Jurat: Do you solemnly (swear/affirm) that this statement is true, (so help you God / on your honor)?

Signer 1 Name and Address:		Signer 2 Name and Address:	

Identification Method:☐ Personally Known ☐ Other ☐ Texas Driver's License ☐ Driver's License ☐ Passport	Identification Method:☐ Personally Known ☐ Other ☐ Texas Driver's License ☐ Driver's License ☐ Passport
Sign Here X _____	Sign Here X _____

Date/Time:	Ref#:

Signing Address:

Document Date	Notarization **A**ck **J**ur **O**th Fee if any	Document Description	Signer Initials	
			1	2
		Deed of Trust / Mortgage		
		Deed - General - Quit Claim - Special Warranty		
		Borrower's Title Affidavit		
		Borrower's Closing Affidavit		
		E&O / Compliance Agreement		
		Occupancy Affidavit		
		Signature Name Affidavit		
		Power of Attorney - Limited / Durable		
		T-47 Residential Real Property Affidavit		
		Mineral Rights Acknowledgement and Agreement		
		Designation of Homestead / Non-Homestead		
		Notice of Penalties for Making False or Misleading Statements		
		Ownership Affidavit		
		Occupancy and Financial Status Affidavit		
		Obligation of Debts Affidavit		
		Release of Claims and Hold Harmless Agreement		
		Affidavit of Marital Status		
		Tax Indemnity		
		Compliance / Correction Agreement		

Notes:

Ack:Do you acknowledge this as your signature and your free act and deed, for the purposes stated herein?
Jurat: Do you solemnly (swear/affirm) that this statement is true, (so help you God / on your honor)?

Signer 1 Name and Address:		Signer 2 Name and Address:	

Identification Method:☐ Personally Known ☐ Other
☐ Texas Driver's License ☐ Driver's License ☐ Passport

Identification Method:☐ Personally Known ☐ Other
☐ Texas Driver's License ☐ Driver's License ☐ Passport

Sign Here

X _____

Sign Here

X _____

Date/Time: Ref#:

Signing Address:

Document Date	Notarization **Ack Jur Oth** Fee if any	Document Description	Signer Initials	
			1	2
		Deed of Trust / Mortgage		
		Deed - General - Quit Claim - Special Warranty		
		Borrower's Title Affidavit		
		Borrower's Closing Affidavit		
		E&O / Compliance Agreement		
		Occupancy Affidavit		
		Signature Name Affidavit		
		Power of Attorney - Limited / Durable		
		T-47 Residential Real Property Affidavit		
		Mineral Rights Acknowledgement and Agreement		
		Designation of Homestead / Non-Homestead		
		Notice of Penalties for Making False or Misleading Statements		
		Ownership Affidavit		
		Occupancy and Financial Status Affidavit		
		Obligation of Debts Affidavit		
		Release of Claims and Hold Harmless Agreement		
		Affidavit of Marital Status		
		Tax Indemnity		
		Compliance / Correction Agreement		

Notes:

Ack:Do you acknowledge this as your signature and your free act and deed, for the purposes stated herein?
Jurat: Do you solemnly (swear/affirm) that this statement is true, (so help you God / on your honor)?

9

Signer 1 Name and Address:		Signer 2 Name and Address:	
Identification Method:☐ Personally Known ☐ Other ☐ Texas Driver's License ☐ Driver's License ☐ Passport		Identification Method:☐ Personally Known ☐ Other ☐ Texas Driver's License ☐ Driver's License ☐ Passport	
Sign Here		*Sign Here*	
X _____		X _____	
Date/Time:		Ref#:	

Signing Address:

Document Date	Notarization **Ack Jur O**th Fee if any	Document Description	Signer Initials	
			1	2
		Deed of Trust / Mortgage		
		Deed - General - Quit Claim - Special Warranty		
		Borrower's Title Affidavit		
		Borrower's Closing Affidavit		
		E&O / Compliance Agreement		
		Occupancy Affidavit		
		Signature Name Affidavit		
		Power of Attorney - Limited / Durable		
		T-47 Residential Real Property Affidavit		
		Mineral Rights Acknowledgement and Agreement		
		Designation of Homestead / Non-Homestead		
		Notice of Penalties for Making False or Misleading Statements		
		Ownership Affidavit		
		Occupancy and Financial Status Affidavit		
		Obligation of Debts Affidavit		
		Release of Claims and Hold Harmless Agreement		
		Affidavit of Marital Status		
		Tax Indemnity		
		Compliance / Correction Agreement		

Notes:

Ack:Do you acknowledge this as your signature and your free act and deed, for the purposes stated herein?
Jurat: Do you solemnly (swear/affirm) that this statement is true, (so help you God / on your honor)?

Signer 1 Name and Address:		Signer 2 Name and Address:	
Identification Method:☐ Personally Known ☐ Other ☐ Texas Driver's License ☐ Driver's License ☐ Passport		Identification Method:☐ Personally Known ☐ Other ☐ Texas Driver's License ☐ Driver's License ☐ Passport	

Sign Here

Sign Here

X _____

X _____

Date/Time: **Ref#:**

Signing Address:

Document Date	Notarization **A**ck **J**ur **O**th Fee if any	Document Description	Signer Initials	
			1	2
		Deed of Trust / Mortgage		
		Deed - General - Quit Claim - Special Warranty		
		Borrower's Title Affidavit		
		Borrower's Closing Affidavit		
		E&O / Compliance Agreement		
		Occupancy Affidavit		
		Signature Name Affidavit		
		Power of Attorney - Limited / Durable		
		T-47 Residential Real Property Affidavit		
		Mineral Rights Acknowledgement and Agreement		
		Designation of Homestead / Non-Homestead		
		Notice of Penalties for Making False or Misleading Statements		
		Ownership Affidavit		
		Occupancy and Financial Status Affidavit		
		Obligation of Debts Affidavit		
		Release of Claims and Hold Harmless Agreement		
		Affidavit of Marital Status		
		Tax Indemnity		
		Compliance / Correction Agreement		

Notes:

Ack:Do you acknowledge this as your signature and your free act and deed, for the purposes stated herein?
Jurat: Do you solemnly (swear/affirm) that this statement is true, (so help you God / on your honor)?

Signer 1 Name and Address:			Signer 2 Name and Address:		
Identification Method:☐ Personally Known ☐ Other ☐ Texas Driver's License ☐ Driver's License ☐ Passport			Identification Method:☐ Personally Known ☐ Other ☐ Texas Driver's License ☐ Driver's License ☐ Passport		
Sign Here			Sign Here		
X _____			X _____		
Date/Time:			Ref#:		
Signing Address:					

Document Date	Notarization **A**ck **J**ur **O**th Fee if any	Document Description		Signer Initials	
				1	2
		Deed of Trust / Mortgage			
		Deed - General - Quit Claim - Special Warranty			
		Borrower's Title Affidavit			
		Borrower's Closing Affidavit			
		E&O / Compliance Agreement			
		Occupancy Affidavit			
		Signature Name Affidavit			
		Power of Attorney - Limited / Durable			
		T-47 Residential Real Property Affidavit			
		Mineral Rights Acknowledgement and Agreement			
		Designation of Homestead / Non-Homestead			
		Notice of Penalties for Making False or Misleading Statements			
		Ownership Affidavit			
		Occupancy and Financial Status Affidavit			
		Obligation of Debts Affidavit			
		Release of Claims and Hold Harmless Agreement			
		Affidavit of Marital Status			
		Tax Indemnity			
		Compliance / Correction Agreement			

Notes:

Ack:Do you acknowledge this as your signature and your free act and deed, for the purposes stated herein?
Jurat: Do you solemnly (swear/affirm) that this statement is true, (so help you God / on your honor)?

12

Signer 1 Name and Address:		Signer 2 Name and Address:	

Identification Method:☐ Personally Known ☐ Other
☐ Texas Driver's License ☐ Driver's License ☐ Passport

Identification Method:☐ Personally Known ☐ Other
☐ Texas Driver's License ☐ Driver's License ☐ Passport

Sign Here

Sign Here

X _____

X _____

Date/Time:

Ref#:

Signing Address:

Document Date	Notarization **Ack Jur Oth** Fee if any	Document Description	Signer Initials	
			1	2
		Deed of Trust / Mortgage		
		Deed - General - Quit Claim - Special Warranty		
		Borrower's Title Affidavit		
		Borrower's Closing Affidavit		
		E&O / Compliance Agreement		
		Occupancy Affidavit		
		Signature Name Affidavit		
		Power of Attorney - Limited / Durable		
		T-47 Residential Real Property Affidavit		
		Mineral Rights Acknowledgement and Agreement		
		Designation of Homestead / Non-Homestead		
		Notice of Penalties for Making False or Misleading Statements		
		Ownership Affidavit		
		Occupancy and Financial Status Affidavit		
		Obligation of Debts Affidavit		
		Release of Claims and Hold Harmless Agreement		
		Affidavit of Marital Status		
		Tax Indemnity		
		Compliance / Correction Agreement		

Notes:

Ack:Do you acknowledge this as your signature and your free act and deed, for the purposes stated herein?
Jurat: Do you solemnly (swear/affirm) that this statement is true, (so help you God / on your honor)?

Signer 1 Name and Address:		Signer 2 Name and Address:	
Identification Method:☐ Personally Known ☐ Other ☐ Texas Driver's License ☐ Driver's License ☐ Passport		Identification Method:☐ Personally Known ☐ Other ☐ Texas Driver's License ☐ Driver's License ☐ Passport	
X _____		X _____	
Date/Time:		Ref#:	

Signing Address:

Document Date	Notarization **A**ck **J**ur **O**th Fee if any	Document Description	Signer Initials	
			1	2
		Deed of Trust / Mortgage		
		Deed - General - Quit Claim - Special Warranty		
		Borrower's Title Affidavit		
		Borrower's Closing Affidavit		
		E&O / Compliance Agreement		
		Occupancy Affidavit		
		Signature Name Affidavit		
		Power of Attorney - Limited / Durable		
		T-47 Residential Real Property Affidavit		
		Mineral Rights Acknowledgement and Agreement		
		Designation of Homestead / Non-Homestead		
		Notice of Penalties for Making False or Misleading Statements		
		Ownership Affidavit		
		Occupancy and Financial Status Affidavit		
		Obligation of Debts Affidavit		
		Release of Claims and Hold Harmless Agreement		
		Affidavit of Marital Status		
		Tax Indemnity		
		Compliance / Correction Agreement		

Notes:

Ack:Do you acknowledge this as your signature and your free act and deed, for the purposes stated herein?
Jurat: Do you solemnly (swear/affirm) that this statement is true, (so help you God / on your honor)?

Signer 1 Name and Address:			Signer 2 Name and Address:		
Identification Method:☐ Personally Known ☐ Other ☐ Texas Driver's License ☐ Driver's License ☐ Passport			Identification Method:☐ Personally Known ☐ Other ☐ Texas Driver's License ☐ Driver's License ☐ Passport		

X _____   X _____

Date/Time: Ref#:

Signing Address:

Document Date	Notarization **Ack Jur Oth** Fee if any	Document Description	Signer Initials	
			1	2
		Deed of Trust / Mortgage		
		Deed - General - Quit Claim - Special Warranty		
		Borrower's Title Affidavit		
		Borrower's Closing Affidavit		
		E&O / Compliance Agreement		
		Occupancy Affidavit		
		Signature Name Affidavit		
		Power of Attorney - Limited / Durable		
		T-47 Residential Real Property Affidavit		
		Mineral Rights Acknowledgement and Agreement		
		Designation of Homestead / Non-Homestead		
		Notice of Penalties for Making False or Misleading Statements		
		Ownership Affidavit		
		Occupancy and Financial Status Affidavit		
		Obligation of Debts Affidavit		
		Release of Claims and Hold Harmless Agreement		
		Affidavit of Marital Status		
		Tax Indemnity		
		Compliance / Correction Agreement		

Notes:

Ack:Do you acknowledge this as your signature and your free act and deed, for the purposes stated herein?
Jurat: Do you solemnly (swear/affirm) that this statement is true, (so help you God / on your honor)?

Signer 1 Name and Address:			Signer 2 Name and Address:		

Identification Method:☐ Personally Known ☐ Other ☐ Texas Driver's License ☐ Driver's License ☐ Passport			Identification Method:☐ Personally Known ☐ Other ☐ Texas Driver's License ☐ Driver's License ☐ Passport		

Sign Here

X _____

Sign Here

X _____

Date/Time: **Ref#:**

Signing Address:

Document Date	Notarization **Ack Jur Oth** Fee if any	Document Description	Signer Initials	
			1	2
		Deed of Trust / Mortgage		
		Deed - General - Quit Claim - Special Warranty		
		Borrower's Title Affidavit		
		Borrower's Closing Affidavit		
		E&O / Compliance Agreement		
		Occupancy Affidavit		
		Signature Name Affidavit		
		Power of Attorney - Limited / Durable		
		T-47 Residential Real Property Affidavit		
		Mineral Rights Acknowledgement and Agreement		
		Designation of Homestead / Non-Homestead		
		Notice of Penalties for Making False or Misleading Statements		
		Ownership Affidavit		
		Occupancy and Financial Status Affidavit		
		Obligation of Debts Affidavit		
		Release of Claims and Hold Harmless Agreement		
		Affidavit of Marital Status		
		Tax Indemnity		
		Compliance / Correction Agreement		

Notes:

Ack: Do you acknowledge this as your signature and your free act and deed, for the purposes stated herein?
Jurat: Do you solemnly (swear/affirm) that this statement is true, (so help you God / on your honor)?

Signer 1 Name and Address:			Signer 2 Name and Address:		

Identification Method: ☐ Personally Known ☐ Other	Identification Method: ☐ Personally Known ☐ Other
☐ Texas Driver's License ☐ Driver's License ☐ Passport	☐ Texas Driver's License ☐ Driver's License ☐ Passport

X _____   X _____

Date/Time: **Ref#:**

Signing Address:

Document Date	Notarization **A**ck **J**ur **O**th Fee if any	Document Description	Signer Initials 1	2
		Deed of Trust / Mortgage		
		Deed - General - Quit Claim - Special Warranty		
		Borrower's Title Affidavit		
		Borrower's Closing Affidavit		
		E&O / Compliance Agreement		
		Occupancy Affidavit		
		Signature Name Affidavit		
		Power of Attorney - Limited / Durable		
		T-47 Residential Real Property Affidavit		
		Mineral Rights Acknowledgement and Agreement		
		Designation of Homestead / Non-Homestead		
		Notice of Penalties for Making False or Misleading Statements		
		Ownership Affidavit		
		Occupancy and Financial Status Affidavit		
		Obligation of Debts Affidavit		
		Release of Claims and Hold Harmless Agreement		
		Affidavit of Marital Status		
		Tax Indemnity		
		Compliance / Correction Agreement		

Notes:

Ack: Do you acknowledge this as your signature and your free act and deed, for the purposes stated herein?
Jurat: Do you solemnly (swear/affirm) that this statement is true, (so help you God / on your honor)?

Signer 1 Name and Address:		Signer 2 Name and Address:	
Identification Method: ☐ Personally Known ☐ Other ☐ Texas Driver's License ☐ Driver's License ☐ Passport		Identification Method: ☐ Personally Known ☐ Other ☐ Texas Driver's License ☐ Driver's License ☐ Passport	
Sign Here X _____		Sign Here X _____	
Date/Time:		Ref#:	

Signing Address:

Document Date	Notarization **Ack Jur Oth** Fee if any	Document Description	Signer Initials	
			1	2
		Deed of Trust / Mortgage		
		Deed - General - Quit Claim - Special Warranty		
		Borrower's Title Affidavit		
		Borrower's Closing Affidavit		
		E&O / Compliance Agreement		
		Occupancy Affidavit		
		Signature Name Affidavit		
		Power of Attorney - Limited / Durable		
		T-47 Residential Real Property Affidavit		
		Mineral Rights Acknowledgement and Agreement		
		Designation of Homestead / Non-Homestead		
		Notice of Penalties for Making False or Misleading Statements		
		Ownership Affidavit		
		Occupancy and Financial Status Affidavit		
		Obligation of Debts Affidavit		
		Release of Claims and Hold Harmless Agreement		
		Affidavit of Marital Status		
		Tax Indemnity		
		Compliance / Correction Agreement		

Notes:

Ack: Do you acknowledge this as your signature and your free act and deed, for the purposes stated herein?
Jurat: Do you solemnly (swear/affirm) that this statement is true, (so help you God / on your honor)?

Signer 1 Name and Address:	Signer 2 Name and Address:
Identification Method:☐ Personally Known ☐ Other ☐ Texas Driver's License ☐ Driver's License ☐ Passport	Identification Method:☐ Personally Known ☐ Other ☐ Texas Driver's License ☐ Driver's License ☐ Passport
X _____	X _____

Date/Time:	Ref#:

Signing Address:

Document Date	Notarization **Ack Jur Oth** Fee if any	Document Description	Signer Initials	
			1	2
		Deed of Trust / Mortgage		
		Deed - General - Quit Claim - Special Warranty		
		Borrower's Title Affidavit		
		Borrower's Closing Affidavit		
		E&O / Compliance Agreement		
		Occupancy Affidavit		
		Signature Name Affidavit		
		Power of Attorney - Limited / Durable		
		T-47 Residential Real Property Affidavit		
		Mineral Rights Acknowledgement and Agreement		
		Designation of Homestead / Non-Homestead		
		Notice of Penalties for Making False or Misleading Statements		
		Ownership Affidavit		
		Occupancy and Financial Status Affidavit		
		Obligation of Debts Affidavit		
		Release of Claims and Hold Harmless Agreement		
		Affidavit of Marital Status		
		Tax Indemnity		
		Compliance / Correction Agreement		

Notes:

Ack:Do you acknowledge this as your signature and your free act and deed, for the purposes stated herein?
Jurat: Do you solemnly (swear/affirm) that this statement is true, (so help you God / on your honor)?

Signer 1 Name and Address:			Signer 2 Name and Address:		
Identification Method: ☐ Personally Known ☐ Other ☐ Texas Driver's License ☐ Driver's License ☐ Passport			Identification Method: ☐ Personally Known ☐ Other ☐ Texas Driver's License ☐ Driver's License ☐ Passport		
Sign Here			Sign Here		
X _____			X _____		
Date/Time:			Ref#:		

Signing Address:

Document Date	Notarization **A**ck **J**ur **O**th Fee if any	Document Description	Signer Initials	
			1	2
		Deed of Trust / Mortgage		
		Deed - General - Quit Claim - Special Warranty		
		Borrower's Title Affidavit		
		Borrower's Closing Affidavit		
		E&O / Compliance Agreement		
		Occupancy Affidavit		
		Signature Name Affidavit		
		Power of Attorney - Limited / Durable		
		T-47 Residential Real Property Affidavit		
		Mineral Rights Acknowledgement and Agreement		
		Designation of Homestead / Non-Homestead		
		Notice of Penalties for Making False or Misleading Statements		
		Ownership Affidavit		
		Occupancy and Financial Status Affidavit		
		Obligation of Debts Affidavit		
		Release of Claims and Hold Harmless Agreement		
		Affidavit of Marital Status		
		Tax Indemnity		
		Compliance / Correction Agreement		

Notes:

Ack: Do you acknowledge this as your signature and your free act and deed, for the purposes stated herein?
Jurat: Do you solemnly (swear/affirm) that this statement is true, (so help you God / on your honor)?

Signer 1 Name and Address:		Signer 2 Name and Address:	

Identification Method: ☐ Personally Known ☐ Other ☐ Texas Driver's License ☐ Driver's License ☐ Passport	Identification Method: ☐ Personally Known ☐ Other ☐ Texas Driver's License ☐ Driver's License ☐ Passport
Sign Here X _____	Sign Here X _____

Date/Time: **Ref#:**

Signing Address:

Document Date	Notarization **Ack Jur Oth** Fee if any	Document Description	Signer Initials 1	2
		Deed of Trust / Mortgage		
		Deed - General - Quit Claim - Special Warranty		
		Borrower's Title Affidavit		
		Borrower's Closing Affidavit		
		E&O / Compliance Agreement		
		Occupancy Affidavit		
		Signature Name Affidavit		
		Power of Attorney - Limited / Durable		
		T-47 Residential Real Property Affidavit		
		Mineral Rights Acknowledgement and Agreement		
		Designation of Homestead / Non-Homestead		
		Notice of Penalties for Making False or Misleading Statements		
		Ownership Affidavit		
		Occupancy and Financial Status Affidavit		
		Obligation of Debts Affidavit		
		Release of Claims and Hold Harmless Agreement		
		Affidavit of Marital Status		
		Tax Indemnity		
		Compliance / Correction Agreement		

Notes:

Ack: Do you acknowledge this as your signature and your free act and deed, for the purposes stated herein?
Jurat: Do you solemnly (swear/affirm) that this statement is true, (so help you God / on your honor)?

Signer 1 Name and Address:		Signer 2 Name and Address:	
Identification Method: ☐ Personally Known ☐ Other ☐ Texas Driver's License ☐ Driver's License ☐ Passport		Identification Method: ☐ Personally Known ☐ Other ☐ Texas Driver's License ☐ Driver's License ☐ Passport	
Sign Here X _____		Sign Here X _____	

Date/Time: Ref#:

Signing Address:

Document Date	Notarization **Ack Jur Oth** Fee if any	Document Description	Signer Initials	
			1	2
		Deed of Trust / Mortgage		
		Deed - General - Quit Claim - Special Warranty		
		Borrower's Title Affidavit		
		Borrower's Closing Affidavit		
		E&O / Compliance Agreement		
		Occupancy Affidavit		
		Signature Name Affidavit		
		Power of Attorney - Limited / Durable		
		T-47 Residential Real Property Affidavit		
		Mineral Rights Acknowledgement and Agreement		
		Designation of Homestead / Non-Homestead		
		Notice of Penalties for Making False or Misleading Statements		
		Ownership Affidavit		
		Occupancy and Financial Status Affidavit		
		Obligation of Debts Affidavit		
		Release of Claims and Hold Harmless Agreement		
		Affidavit of Marital Status		
		Tax Indemnity		
		Compliance / Correction Agreement		

Notes:

Ack: Do you acknowledge this as your signature and your free act and deed, for the purposes stated herein?
Jurat: Do you solemnly (swear/affirm) that this statement is true, (so help you God / on your honor)?

Signer 1 Name and Address:		Signer 2 Name and Address:	

Identification Method: ☐ Personally Known ☐ Other
☐ Texas Driver's License ☐ Driver's License ☐ Passport

Identification Method: ☐ Personally Known ☐ Other
☐ Texas Driver's License ☐ Driver's License ☐ Passport

X _____   X _____

Date/Time: Ref#:

Signing Address:

Document Date	Notarization **A**ck **J**ur **O**th Fee if any	Document Description	Signer Initials 1	2
		Deed of Trust / Mortgage		
		Deed - General - Quit Claim - Special Warranty		
		Borrower's Title Affidavit		
		Borrower's Closing Affidavit		
		E&O / Compliance Agreement		
		Occupancy Affidavit		
		Signature Name Affidavit		
		Power of Attorney - Limited / Durable		
		T-47 Residential Real Property Affidavit		
		Mineral Rights Acknowledgement and Agreement		
		Designation of Homestead / Non-Homestead		
		Notice of Penalties for Making False or Misleading Statements		
		Ownership Affidavit		
		Occupancy and Financial Status Affidavit		
		Obligation of Debts Affidavit		
		Release of Claims and Hold Harmless Agreement		
		Affidavit of Marital Status		
		Tax Indemnity		
		Compliance / Correction Agreement		

Notes:

Ack: Do you acknowledge this as your signature and your free act and deed, for the purposes stated herein?
Jurat: Do you solemnly (swear/affirm) that this statement is true, (so help you God / on your honor)?

Signer 1 Name and Address:		Signer 2 Name and Address:	
Identification Method:☐ Personally Known ☐ Other ☐ Texas Driver's License ☐ Driver's License ☐ Passport		Identification Method:☐ Personally Known ☐ Other ☐ Texas Driver's License ☐ Driver's License ☐ Passport	
Sign Here		Sign Here	
X _____		X _____	
Date/Time:		Ref#:	

Signing Address:

Document Date	Notarization **A**ck **J**ur **O**th Fee if any	Document Description	Signer Initials	
			1	2
		Deed of Trust / Mortgage		
		Deed - General - Quit Claim - Special Warranty		
		Borrower's Title Affidavit		
		Borrower's Closing Affidavit		
		E&O / Compliance Agreement		
		Occupancy Affidavit		
		Signature Name Affidavit		
		Power of Attorney - Limited / Durable		
		T-47 Residential Real Property Affidavit		
		Mineral Rights Acknowledgement and Agreement		
		Designation of Homestead / Non-Homestead		
		Notice of Penalties for Making False or Misleading Statements		
		Ownership Affidavit		
		Occupancy and Financial Status Affidavit		
		Obligation of Debts Affidavit		
		Release of Claims and Hold Harmless Agreement		
		Affidavit of Marital Status		
		Tax Indemnity		
		Compliance / Correction Agreement		

Notes:

Ack:Do you acknowledge this as your signature and your free act and deed, for the purposes stated herein?
Jurat: Do you solemnly (swear/affirm) that this statement is true, (so help you God / on your honor)?

Signer 1 Name and Address:		Signer 2 Name and Address:	

Identification Method: ☐ Personally Known ☐ Other ☐ Texas Driver's License ☐ Driver's License ☐ Passport	Identification Method: ☐ Personally Known ☐ Other ☐ Texas Driver's License ☐ Driver's License ☐ Passport
X _____ Sign Here	X _____ Sign Here

Date/Time: Ref#:

Signing Address:

Document Date	Notarization **Ack Jur Oth** Fee if any	Document Description	Signer Initials 1	2
		Deed of Trust / Mortgage		
		Deed - General - Quit Claim - Special Warranty		
		Borrower's Title Affidavit		
		Borrower's Closing Affidavit		
		E&O / Compliance Agreement		
		Occupancy Affidavit		
		Signature Name Affidavit		
		Power of Attorney - Limited / Durable		
		T-47 Residential Real Property Affidavit		
		Mineral Rights Acknowledgement and Agreement		
		Designation of Homestead / Non-Homestead		
		Notice of Penalties for Making False or Misleading Statements		
		Ownership Affidavit		
		Occupancy and Financial Status Affidavit		
		Obligation of Debts Affidavit		
		Release of Claims and Hold Harmless Agreement		
		Affidavit of Marital Status		
		Tax Indemnity		
		Compliance / Correction Agreement		

Notes:

Ack: Do you acknowledge this as your signature and your free act and deed, for the purposes stated herein?
Jurat: Do you solemnly (swear/affirm) that this statement is true, (so help you God / on your honor)?

Signer 1 Name and Address:		Signer 2 Name and Address:	

Identification Method:☐ Personally Known ☐ Other
☐ Texas Driver's License ☐ Driver's License ☐ Passport

Identification Method:☐ Personally Known ☐ Other
☐ Texas Driver's License ☐ Driver's License ☐ Passport

Sign Here   *Sign Here*

X _____   X _____

Date/Time: _____   Ref#: _____

Signing Address:

Document Date	Notarization **Ack Jur O**th Fee if any	Document Description	Signer Initials	
			1	2
		Deed of Trust / Mortgage		
		Deed - General - Quit Claim - Special Warranty		
		Borrower's Title Affidavit		
		Borrower's Closing Affidavit		
		E&O / Compliance Agreement		
		Occupancy Affidavit		
		Signature Name Affidavit		
		Power of Attorney - Limited / Durable		
		T-47 Residential Real Property Affidavit		
		Mineral Rights Acknowledgement and Agreement		
		Designation of Homestead / Non-Homestead		
		Notice of Penalties for Making False or Misleading Statements		
		Ownership Affidavit		
		Occupancy and Financial Status Affidavit		
		Obligation of Debts Affidavit		
		Release of Claims and Hold Harmless Agreement		
		Affidavit of Marital Status		
		Tax Indemnity		
		Compliance / Correction Agreement		

Notes:

Ack:Do you acknowledge this as your signature and your free act and deed, for the purposes stated herein?
Jurat: Do you solemnly (swear/affirm) that this statement is true, (so help you God / on your honor)?

Signer 1 Name and Address:			Signer 2 Name and Address:	

Identification Method: ☐ Personally Known ☐ Other
☐ Texas Driver's License ☐ Driver's License ☐ Passport

Identification Method: ☐ Personally Known ☐ Other
☐ Texas Driver's License ☐ Driver's License ☐ Passport

Sign Here

X _____

Sign Here

X _____

Date/Time: _____   Ref#: _____

Signing Address:

Document Date	Notarization **A**ck **J**ur **O**th Fee if any	Document Description	Signer Initials	
			1	2
		Deed of Trust / Mortgage		
		Deed - General - Quit Claim - Special Warranty		
		Borrower's Title Affidavit		
		Borrower's Closing Affidavit		
		E&O / Compliance Agreement		
		Occupancy Affidavit		
		Signature Name Affidavit		
		Power of Attorney - Limited / Durable		
		T-47 Residential Real Property Affidavit		
		Mineral Rights Acknowledgement and Agreement		
		Designation of Homestead / Non-Homestead		
		Notice of Penalties for Making False or Misleading Statements		
		Ownership Affidavit		
		Occupancy and Financial Status Affidavit		
		Obligation of Debts Affidavit		
		Release of Claims and Hold Harmless Agreement		
		Affidavit of Marital Status		
		Tax Indemnity		
		Compliance / Correction Agreement		

Notes:

Ack: Do you acknowledge this as your signature and your free act and deed, for the purposes stated herein?
Jurat: Do you solemnly (swear/affirm) that this statement is true, (so help you God / on your honor)?

Signer 1 Name and Address:			Signer 2 Name and Address:		

Identification Method:☐ Personally Known ☐ Other
☐ Texas Driver's License ☐ Driver's License ☐ Passport

Identification Method:☐ Personally Known ☐ Other
☐ Texas Driver's License ☐ Driver's License ☐ Passport

Sign Here

Sign Here

X _____

X _____

Date/Time:

Ref#:

Signing Address:

Document Date	Notarization **Ack Jur Oth** Fee if any	Document Description	Signer Initials	
			1	2
		Deed of Trust / Mortgage		
		Deed - General - Quit Claim - Special Warranty		
		Borrower's Title Affidavit		
		Borrower's Closing Affidavit		
		E&O / Compliance Agreement		
		Occupancy Affidavit		
		Signature Name Affidavit		
		Power of Attorney - Limited / Durable		
		T-47 Residential Real Property Affidavit		
		Mineral Rights Acknowledgement and Agreement		
		Designation of Homestead / Non-Homestead		
		Notice of Penalties for Making False or Misleading Statements		
		Ownership Affidavit		
		Occupancy and Financial Status Affidavit		
		Obligation of Debts Affidavit		
		Release of Claims and Hold Harmless Agreement		
		Affidavit of Marital Status		
		Tax Indemnity		
		Compliance / Correction Agreement		

Notes:

Ack:Do you acknowledge this as your signature and your free act and deed, for the purposes stated herein?
Jurat: Do you solemnly (swear/affirm) that this statement is true, (so help you God / on your honor)?
28

Signer 1 Name and Address:		Signer 2 Name and Address:

Identification Method:☐ Personally Known ☐ Other
☐ Texas Driver's License ☐ Driver's License ☐ Passport

Identification Method:☐ Personally Known ☐ Other
☐ Texas Driver's License ☐ Driver's License ☐ Passport

Sign Here

Sign Here

X _____

X _____

Date/Time: Ref#:

Signing Address:

Document Date	Notarization **A**ck **J**ur **O**th Fee if any	Document Description	Signer Initials	
			1	2
		Deed of Trust / Mortgage		
		Deed - General - Quit Claim - Special Warranty		
		Borrower's Title Affidavit		
		Borrower's Closing Affidavit		
		E&O / Compliance Agreement		
		Occupancy Affidavit		
		Signature Name Affidavit		
		Power of Attorney - Limited / Durable		
		T-47 Residential Real Property Affidavit		
		Mineral Rights Acknowledgement and Agreement		
		Designation of Homestead / Non-Homestead		
		Notice of Penalties for Making False or Misleading Statements		
		Ownership Affidavit		
		Occupancy and Financial Status Affidavit		
		Obligation of Debts Affidavit		
		Release of Claims and Hold Harmless Agreement		
		Affidavit of Marital Status		
		Tax Indemnity		
		Compliance / Correction Agreement		

Notes:

Ack:Do you acknowledge this as your signature and your free act and deed, for the purposes stated herein?
Jurat: Do you solemnly (swear/affirm) that this statement is true, (so help you God / on your honor)?

Signer 1 Name and Address:		Signer 2 Name and Address:	
Identification Method:☐ Personally Known ☐ Other ☐ Texas Driver's License ☐ Driver's License ☐ Passport		Identification Method:☐ Personally Known ☐ Other ☐ Texas Driver's License ☐ Driver's License ☐ Passport	
Sign Here X _____		Sign Here X _____	
Date/Time:		Ref#:	
Signing Address:			

Document Date	Notarization **A**ck **J**ur **O**th Fee if any	Document Description	Signer Initials	
			1	2
		Deed of Trust / Mortgage		
		Deed - General - Quit Claim - Special Warranty		
		Borrower's Title Affidavit		
		Borrower's Closing Affidavit		
		E&O / Compliance Agreement		
		Occupancy Affidavit		
		Signature Name Affidavit		
		Power of Attorney - Limited / Durable		
		T-47 Residential Real Property Affidavit		
		Mineral Rights Acknowledgement and Agreement		
		Designation of Homestead / Non-Homestead		
		Notice of Penalties for Making False or Misleading Statements		
		Ownership Affidavit		
		Occupancy and Financial Status Affidavit		
		Obligation of Debts Affidavit		
		Release of Claims and Hold Harmless Agreement		
		Affidavit of Marital Status		
		Tax Indemnity		
		Compliance / Correction Agreement		

Notes:

Ack:Do you acknowledge this as your signature and your free act and deed, for the purposes stated herein?
Jurat: Do you solemnly (swear/affirm) that this statement is true, (so help you God / on your honor)?

Signer 1 Name and Address:			Signer 2 Name and Address:		

Identification Method: ☐ Personally Known ☐ Other
☐ Texas Driver's License ☐ Driver's License ☐ Passport

Identification Method: ☐ Personally Known ☐ Other
☐ Texas Driver's License ☐ Driver's License ☐ Passport

X _____ X _____

Date/Time: Ref#:

Signing Address:

Document Date	Notarization **A**ck **J**ur **O**th Fee if any	Document Description	Signer Initials	
			1	2
		Deed of Trust / Mortgage		
		Deed - General - Quit Claim - Special Warranty		
		Borrower's Title Affidavit		
		Borrower's Closing Affidavit		
		E&O / Compliance Agreement		
		Occupancy Affidavit		
		Signature Name Affidavit		
		Power of Attorney - Limited / Durable		
		T-47 Residential Real Property Affidavit		
		Mineral Rights Acknowledgement and Agreement		
		Designation of Homestead / Non-Homestead		
		Notice of Penalties for Making False or Misleading Statements		
		Ownership Affidavit		
		Occupancy and Financial Status Affidavit		
		Obligation of Debts Affidavit		
		Release of Claims and Hold Harmless Agreement		
		Affidavit of Marital Status		
		Tax Indemnity		
		Compliance / Correction Agreement		

Notes:

Ack:Do you acknowledge this as your signature and your free act and deed, for the purposes stated herein?
Jurat: Do you solemnly (swear/affirm) that this statement is true, (so help you God / on your honor)?

Signer 1 Name and Address:		Signer 2 Name and Address:	

Identification Method:☐ Personally Known ☐ Other ☐ Texas Driver's License ☐ Driver's License ☐ Passport	Identification Method:☐ Personally Known ☐ Other ☐ Texas Driver's License ☐ Driver's License ☐ Passport

Sign Here

Sign Here

X _____   X _____

Date/Time: Ref#:

Signing Address:

Document Date	Notarization **Ack Jur O**th Fee if any	Document Description	Signer Initials	
			1	2
		Deed of Trust / Mortgage		
		Deed - General - Quit Claim - Special Warranty		
		Borrower's Title Affidavit		
		Borrower's Closing Affidavit		
		E&O / Compliance Agreement		
		Occupancy Affidavit		
		Signature Name Affidavit		
		Power of Attorney - Limited / Durable		
		T-47 Residential Real Property Affidavit		
		Mineral Rights Acknowledgement and Agreement		
		Designation of Homestead / Non-Homestead		
		Notice of Penalties for Making False or Misleading Statements		
		Ownership Affidavit		
		Occupancy and Financial Status Affidavit		
		Obligation of Debts Affidavit		
		Release of Claims and Hold Harmless Agreement		
		Affidavit of Marital Status		
		Tax Indemnity		
		Compliance / Correction Agreement		

Notes:

Ack:Do you acknowledge this as your signature and your free act and deed, for the purposes stated herein?
Jurat: Do you solemnly (swear/affirm) that this statement is true, (so help you God / on your honor)?

Signer 1 Name and Address:		Signer 2 Name and Address:	

Identification Method: ☐ Personally Known ☐ Other
☐ Texas Driver's License ☐ Driver's License ☐ Passport

Identification Method: ☐ Personally Known ☐ Other
☐ Texas Driver's License ☐ Driver's License ☐ Passport

Sign Here   Sign Here

X _____   X _____

Date/Time: Ref#:

Signing Address:

Document Date	Notarization **A**ck **J**ur **O**th Fee if any	Document Description	Signer Initials	
			1	2
		Deed of Trust / Mortgage		
		Deed - General - Quit Claim - Special Warranty		
		Borrower's Title Affidavit		
		Borrower's Closing Affidavit		
		E&O / Compliance Agreement		
		Occupancy Affidavit		
		Signature Name Affidavit		
		Power of Attorney - Limited / Durable		
		T-47 Residential Real Property Affidavit		
		Mineral Rights Acknowledgement and Agreement		
		Designation of Homestead / Non-Homestead		
		Notice of Penalties for Making False or Misleading Statements		
		Ownership Affidavit		
		Occupancy and Financial Status Affidavit		
		Obligation of Debts Affidavit		
		Release of Claims and Hold Harmless Agreement		
		Affidavit of Marital Status		
		Tax Indemnity		
		Compliance / Correction Agreement		

Notes:

Ack: Do you acknowledge this as your signature and your free act and deed, for the purposes stated herein?
Jurat: Do you solemnly (swear/affirm) that this statement is true, (so help you God / on your honor)?

Signer 1 Name and Address:		Signer 2 Name and Address:	

Identification Method: ☐ Personally Known ☐ Other ☐ Texas Driver's License ☐ Driver's License ☐ Passport	Identification Method: ☐ Personally Known ☐ Other ☐ Texas Driver's License ☐ Driver's License ☐ Passport
Sign Here X _____	Sign Here X _____

Date/Time:	Ref#:

Signing Address:

Document Date	Notarization **Ack Jur O**th Fee if any	Document Description	Signer Initials	
			1	2
		Deed of Trust / Mortgage		
		Deed - General - Quit Claim - Special Warranty		
		Borrower's Title Affidavit		
		Borrower's Closing Affidavit		
		E&O / Compliance Agreement		
		Occupancy Affidavit		
		Signature Name Affidavit		
		Power of Attorney - Limited / Durable		
		T-47 Residential Real Property Affidavit		
		Mineral Rights Acknowledgement and Agreement		
		Designation of Homestead / Non-Homestead		
		Notice of Penalties for Making False or Misleading Statements		
		Ownership Affidavit		
		Occupancy and Financial Status Affidavit		
		Obligation of Debts Affidavit		
		Release of Claims and Hold Harmless Agreement		
		Affidavit of Marital Status		
		Tax Indemnity		
		Compliance / Correction Agreement		

Notes:

Ack: Do you acknowledge this as your signature and your free act and deed, for the purposes stated herein?
Jurat: Do you solemnly (swear/affirm) that this statement is true, (so help you God / on your honor)?

Signer 1 Name and Address:		Signer 2 Name and Address:	

Identification Method: ☐ Personally Known ☐ Other ☐ Texas Driver's License ☐ Driver's License ☐ Passport	Identification Method: ☐ Personally Known ☐ Other ☐ Texas Driver's License ☐ Driver's License ☐ Passport

Sign Here

Sign Here

X _____   X _____

Date/Time: Ref#:

Signing Address:

Document Date	Notarization **A**ck **J**ur **O**th Fee if any	Document Description	Signer Initials	
			1	2
		Deed of Trust / Mortgage		
		Deed - General - Quit Claim - Special Warranty		
		Borrower's Title Affidavit		
		Borrower's Closing Affidavit		
		E&O / Compliance Agreement		
		Occupancy Affidavit		
		Signature Name Affidavit		
		Power of Attorney - Limited / Durable		
		T-47 Residential Real Property Affidavit		
		Mineral Rights Acknowledgement and Agreement		
		Designation of Homestead / Non-Homestead		
		Notice of Penalties for Making False or Misleading Statements		
		Ownership Affidavit		
		Occupancy and Financial Status Affidavit		
		Obligation of Debts Affidavit		
		Release of Claims and Hold Harmless Agreement		
		Affidavit of Marital Status		
		Tax Indemnity		
		Compliance / Correction Agreement		

Notes:

Ack:Do you acknowledge this as your signature and your free act and deed, for the purposes stated herein?
Jurat: Do you solemnly (swear/affirm) that this statement is true, (so help you God / on your honor)?

Signer 1 Name and Address:				Signer 2 Name and Address:		

Identification Method:☐ Personally Known ☐ Other	Identification Method:☐ Personally Known ☐ Other
☐ Texas Driver's License ☐ Driver's License ☐ Passport	☐ Texas Driver's License ☐ Driver's License ☐ Passport

Sign Here   Sign Here

X _____   X _____

Date/Time: Ref#:

Signing Address:

Document Date	Notarization **Ack Jur Oth** Fee if any	Document Description	Signer Initials	
			1	2
		Deed of Trust / Mortgage		
		Deed - General - Quit Claim - Special Warranty		
		Borrower's Title Affidavit		
		Borrower's Closing Affidavit		
		E&O / Compliance Agreement		
		Occupancy Affidavit		
		Signature Name Affidavit		
		Power of Attorney - Limited / Durable		
		T-47 Residential Real Property Affidavit		
		Mineral Rights Acknowledgement and Agreement		
		Designation of Homestead / Non-Homestead		
		Notice of Penalties for Making False or Misleading Statements		
		Ownership Affidavit		
		Occupancy and Financial Status Affidavit		
		Obligation of Debts Affidavit		
		Release of Claims and Hold Harmless Agreement		
		Affidavit of Marital Status		
		Tax Indemnity		
		Compliance / Correction Agreement		

Notes:

Ack:Do you acknowledge this as your signature and your free act and deed, for the purposes stated herein?
Jurat: Do you solemnly (swear/affirm) that this statement is true, (so help you God / on your honor)?

Signer 1 Name and Address:		Signer 2 Name and Address:	

Identification Method:☐ Personally Known ☐ Other
☐ Texas Driver's License ☐ Driver's License ☐ Passport

Identification Method:☐ Personally Known ☐ Other
☐ Texas Driver's License ☐ Driver's License ☐ Passport

Sign Here

X _____

Sign Here

X _____

Date/Time: Ref#:

Signing Address:

Document Date	Notarization **Ack Jur Oth** Fee if any	Document Description	Signer Initials 1	2
		Deed of Trust / Mortgage		
		Deed - General - Quit Claim - Special Warranty		
		Borrower's Title Affidavit		
		Borrower's Closing Affidavit		
		E&O / Compliance Agreement		
		Occupancy Affidavit		
		Signature Name Affidavit		
		Power of Attorney - Limited / Durable		
		T-47 Residential Real Property Affidavit		
		Mineral Rights Acknowledgement and Agreement		
		Designation of Homestead / Non-Homestead		
		Notice of Penalties for Making False or Misleading Statements		
		Ownership Affidavit		
		Occupancy and Financial Status Affidavit		
		Obligation of Debts Affidavit		
		Release of Claims and Hold Harmless Agreement		
		Affidavit of Marital Status		
		Tax Indemnity		
		Compliance / Correction Agreement		

Notes:

Ack:Do you acknowledge this as your signature and your free act and deed, for the purposes stated herein?
Jurat: Do you solemnly (swear/affirm) that this statement is true, (so help you God / on your honor)?

Signer 1 Name and Address:		Signer 2 Name and Address:	

Identification Method:☐ Personally Known ☐ Other ☐ Texas Driver's License ☐ Driver's License ☐ Passport	Identification Method:☐ Personally Known ☐ Other ☐ Texas Driver's License ☐ Driver's License ☐ Passport
X _____	X _____

Date/Time: Ref#:

Signing Address:

Document Date	Notarization **Ack Jur O**th Fee if any	Document Description	Signer Initials	
			1	2
		Deed of Trust / Mortgage		
		Deed - General - Quit Claim - Special Warranty		
		Borrower's Title Affidavit		
		Borrower's Closing Affidavit		
		E&O / Compliance Agreement		
		Occupancy Affidavit		
		Signature Name Affidavit		
		Power of Attorney - Limited / Durable		
		T-47 Residential Real Property Affidavit		
		Mineral Rights Acknowledgement and Agreement		
		Designation of Homestead / Non-Homestead		
		Notice of Penalties for Making False or Misleading Statements		
		Ownership Affidavit		
		Occupancy and Financial Status Affidavit		
		Obligation of Debts Affidavit		
		Release of Claims and Hold Harmless Agreement		
		Affidavit of Marital Status		
		Tax Indemnity		
		Compliance / Correction Agreement		

Notes:

Ack:Do you acknowledge this as your signature and your free act and deed, for the purposes stated herein?
Jurat: Do you solemnly (swear/affirm) that this statement is true, (so help you God / on your honor)?

Signer 1 Name and Address:		Signer 2 Name and Address:	

Identification Method: ☐ Personally Known ☐ Other	☐ Texas Driver's License ☐ Driver's License ☐ Passport	Identification Method: ☐ Personally Known ☐ Other	☐ Texas Driver's License ☐ Driver's License ☐ Passport

Sign Here

X _____

Sign Here

X _____

Date/Time: Ref#:

Signing Address:

Document Date	Notarization **Ack Jur Oth** Fee if any	Document Description	Signer Initials	
			1	2
		Deed of Trust / Mortgage		
		Deed - General - Quit Claim - Special Warranty		
		Borrower's Title Affidavit		
		Borrower's Closing Affidavit		
		E&O / Compliance Agreement		
		Occupancy Affidavit		
		Signature Name Affidavit		
		Power of Attorney - Limited / Durable		
		T-47 Residential Real Property Affidavit		
		Mineral Rights Acknowledgement and Agreement		
		Designation of Homestead / Non-Homestead		
		Notice of Penalties for Making False or Misleading Statements		
		Ownership Affidavit		
		Occupancy and Financial Status Affidavit		
		Obligation of Debts Affidavit		
		Release of Claims and Hold Harmless Agreement		
		Affidavit of Marital Status		
		Tax Indemnity		
		Compliance / Correction Agreement		

Notes:

Ack: Do you acknowledge this as your signature and your free act and deed, for the purposes stated herein?
Jurat: Do you solemnly (swear/affirm) that this statement is true, (so help you God / on your honor)?

| Signer 1 Name and Address: | | Signer 2 Name and Address: | |

Signer 1 Name and Address:	Signer 2 Name and Address:
Identification Method:☐ Personally Known ☐ Other ☐ Texas Driver's License ☐ Driver's License ☐ Passport	Identification Method:☐ Personally Known ☐ Other ☐ Texas Driver's License ☐ Driver's License ☐ Passport
Sign Here X _____	Sign Here X _____
Date/Time:	Ref#:

Signing Address:

Document Date	Notarization **Ack Jur O**th Fee if any	Document Description	Signer Initials	
			1	2
		Deed of Trust / Mortgage		
		Deed - General - Quit Claim - Special Warranty		
		Borrower's Title Affidavit		
		Borrower's Closing Affidavit		
		E&O / Compliance Agreement		
		Occupancy Affidavit		
		Signature Name Affidavit		
		Power of Attorney - Limited / Durable		
		T-47 Residential Real Property Affidavit		
		Mineral Rights Acknowledgement and Agreement		
		Designation of Homestead / Non-Homestead		
		Notice of Penalties for Making False or Misleading Statements		
		Ownership Affidavit		
		Occupancy and Financial Status Affidavit		
		Obligation of Debts Affidavit		
		Release of Claims and Hold Harmless Agreement		
		Affidavit of Marital Status		
		Tax Indemnity		
		Compliance / Correction Agreement		

Notes:

Ack:Do you acknowledge this as your signature and your free act and deed, for the purposes stated herein?
Jurat: Do you solemnly (swear/affirm) that this statement is true, (so help you God / on your honor)?

Signer 1 Name and Address:				Signer 2 Name and Address:		

Identification Method:☐ Personally Known ☐ Other
☐ Texas Driver's License ☐ Driver's License ☐ Passport

Identification Method:☐ Personally Known ☐ Other
☐ Texas Driver's License ☐ Driver's License ☐ Passport

X _____

X _____

Date/Time: Ref#:

Signing Address:

Document Date	Notarization **A**ck **J**ur **O**th Fee if any	Document Description	Signer Initials	
			1	2
		Deed of Trust / Mortgage		
		Deed - General - Quit Claim - Special Warranty		
		Borrower's Title Affidavit		
		Borrower's Closing Affidavit		
		E&O / Compliance Agreement		
		Occupancy Affidavit		
		Signature Name Affidavit		
		Power of Attorney - Limited / Durable		
		T-47 Residential Real Property Affidavit		
		Mineral Rights Acknowledgement and Agreement		
		Designation of Homestead / Non-Homestead		
		Notice of Penalties for Making False or Misleading Statements		
		Ownership Affidavit		
		Occupancy and Financial Status Affidavit		
		Obligation of Debts Affidavit		
		Release of Claims and Hold Harmless Agreement		
		Affidavit of Marital Status		
		Tax Indemnity		
		Compliance / Correction Agreement		

Notes:

Ack:Do you acknowledge this as your signature and your free act and deed, for the purposes stated herein?
Jurat: Do you solemnly (swear/affirm) that this statement is true, (so help you God / on your honor)?

Signer 1 Name and Address:		Signer 2 Name and Address:	

Identification Method: ☐ Personally Known ☐ Other
☐ Texas Driver's License ☐ Driver's License ☐ Passport

Identification Method: ☐ Personally Known ☐ Other
☐ Texas Driver's License ☐ Driver's License ☐ Passport

Sign Here

X _____

Sign Here

X _____

Date/Time: Ref#:

Signing Address:

Document Date	Notarization **A**ck **J**ur **O**th Fee if any	Document Description	Signer Initials	
			1	2
		Deed of Trust / Mortgage		
		Deed - General - Quit Claim - Special Warranty		
		Borrower's Title Affidavit		
		Borrower's Closing Affidavit		
		E&O / Compliance Agreement		
		Occupancy Affidavit		
		Signature Name Affidavit		
		Power of Attorney - Limited / Durable		
		T-47 Residential Real Property Affidavit		
		Mineral Rights Acknowledgement and Agreement		
		Designation of Homestead / Non-Homestead		
		Notice of Penalties for Making False or Misleading Statements		
		Ownership Affidavit		
		Occupancy and Financial Status Affidavit		
		Obligation of Debts Affidavit		
		Release of Claims and Hold Harmless Agreement		
		Affidavit of Marital Status		
		Tax Indemnity		
		Compliance / Correction Agreement		

Notes:

Ack:Do you acknowledge this as your signature and your free act and deed, for the purposes stated herein?
Jurat: Do you solemnly (swear/affirm) that this statement is true, (so help you God / on your honor)?

42

Signer 1 Name and Address:		Signer 2 Name and Address:	

Identification Method:☐ Personally Known ☐ Other
☐ Texas Driver's License ☐ Driver's License ☐ Passport

Identification Method:☐ Personally Known ☐ Other
☐ Texas Driver's License ☐ Driver's License ☐ Passport

Sign Here

Sign Here

X _____   X _____

Date/Time: Ref#:

Signing Address:

Document Date	Notarization **Ack Jur Oth** Fee if any	Document Description	Signer Initials	
			1	2
		Deed of Trust / Mortgage		
		Deed - General - Quit Claim - Special Warranty		
		Borrower's Title Affidavit		
		Borrower's Closing Affidavit		
		E&O / Compliance Agreement		
		Occupancy Affidavit		
		Signature Name Affidavit		
		Power of Attorney - Limited / Durable		
		T-47 Residential Real Property Affidavit		
		Mineral Rights Acknowledgement and Agreement		
		Designation of Homestead / Non-Homestead		
		Notice of Penalties for Making False or Misleading Statements		
		Ownership Affidavit		
		Occupancy and Financial Status Affidavit		
		Obligation of Debts Affidavit		
		Release of Claims and Hold Harmless Agreement		
		Affidavit of Marital Status		
		Tax Indemnity		
		Compliance / Correction Agreement		

Notes:

Ack:Do you acknowledge this as your signature and your free act and deed, for the purposes stated herein?
Jurat: Do you solemnly (swear/affirm) that this statement is true, (so help you God / on your honor)?

Signer 1 Name and Address:		Signer 2 Name and Address:	
Identification Method:☐ Personally Known ☐ Other ☐ Texas Driver's License ☐ Driver's License ☐ Passport		Identification Method:☐ Personally Known ☐ Other ☐ Texas Driver's License ☐ Driver's License ☐ Passport	

Sign Here

Sign Here

X _____ X _____

Date/Time:	Ref#:

Signing Address:

Document Date	Notarization **Ack Jur O**th Fee if any	Document Description	Signer Initials	
			1	2
		Deed of Trust / Mortgage		
		Deed - General - Quit Claim - Special Warranty		
		Borrower's Title Affidavit		
		Borrower's Closing Affidavit		
		E&O / Compliance Agreement		
		Occupancy Affidavit		
		Signature Name Affidavit		
		Power of Attorney - Limited / Durable		
		T-47 Residential Real Property Affidavit		
		Mineral Rights Acknowledgement and Agreement		
		Designation of Homestead / Non-Homestead		
		Notice of Penalties for Making False or Misleading Statements		
		Ownership Affidavit		
		Occupancy and Financial Status Affidavit		
		Obligation of Debts Affidavit		
		Release of Claims and Hold Harmless Agreement		
		Affidavit of Marital Status		
		Tax Indemnity		
		Compliance / Correction Agreement		

Notes:

Ack:Do you acknowledge this as your signature and your free act and deed, for the purposes stated herein?
Jurat: Do you solemnly (swear/affirm) that this statement is true, (so help you God / on your honor)?

Signer 1 Name and Address:		Signer 2 Name and Address:	

Identification Method:☐ Personally Known ☐ Other
☐ Texas Driver's License ☐ Driver's License ☐ Passport

Identification Method:☐ Personally Known ☐ Other
☐ Texas Driver's License ☐ Driver's License ☐ Passport

Sign Here

X _____

Sign Here

X _____

Date/Time: **Ref#:**

Signing Address:

Document Date	Notarization **A**ck **J**ur **O**th Fee if any	Document Description	Signer Initials 1	2
		Deed of Trust / Mortgage		
		Deed - General - Quit Claim - Special Warranty		
		Borrower's Title Affidavit		
		Borrower's Closing Affidavit		
		E&O / Compliance Agreement		
		Occupancy Affidavit		
		Signature Name Affidavit		
		Power of Attorney - Limited / Durable		
		T-47 Residential Real Property Affidavit		
		Mineral Rights Acknowledgement and Agreement		
		Designation of Homestead / Non-Homestead		
		Notice of Penalties for Making False or Misleading Statements		
		Ownership Affidavit		
		Occupancy and Financial Status Affidavit		
		Obligation of Debts Affidavit		
		Release of Claims and Hold Harmless Agreement		
		Affidavit of Marital Status		
		Tax Indemnity		
		Compliance / Correction Agreement		

Notes:

Ack:Do you acknowledge this as your signature and your free act and deed, for the purposes stated herein?
Jurat: Do you solemnly (swear/affirm) that this statement is true, (so help you God / on your honor)?

Signer 1 Name and Address:		Signer 2 Name and Address:	

Identification Method: ☐ Personally Known ☐ Other ☐ Texas Driver's License ☐ Driver's License ☐ Passport	Identification Method: ☐ Personally Known ☐ Other ☐ Texas Driver's License ☐ Driver's License ☐ Passport

Sign Here

X _____

Sign Here

X _____

Date/Time: **Ref#:**

Signing Address:

Document Date	Notarization **A**ck **J**ur **O**th Fee if any	Document Description	Signer Initials	
			1	2
		Deed of Trust / Mortgage		
		Deed - General - Quit Claim - Special Warranty		
		Borrower's Title Affidavit		
		Borrower's Closing Affidavit		
		E&O / Compliance Agreement		
		Occupancy Affidavit		
		Signature Name Affidavit		
		Power of Attorney - Limited / Durable		
		T-47 Residential Real Property Affidavit		
		Mineral Rights Acknowledgement and Agreement		
		Designation of Homestead / Non-Homestead		
		Notice of Penalties for Making False or Misleading Statements		
		Ownership Affidavit		
		Occupancy and Financial Status Affidavit		
		Obligation of Debts Affidavit		
		Release of Claims and Hold Harmless Agreement		
		Affidavit of Marital Status		
		Tax Indemnity		
		Compliance / Correction Agreement		

Notes:

Ack:Do you acknowledge this as your signature and your free act and deed, for the purposes stated herein?
Jurat: Do you solemnly (swear/affirm) that this statement is true, (so help you God / on your honor)?

Signer 1 Name and Address:		Signer 2 Name and Address:	

Identification Method:☐ Personally Known ☐ Other
☐ Texas Driver's License ☐ Driver's License ☐ Passport

Identification Method:☐ Personally Known ☐ Other
☐ Texas Driver's License ☐ Driver's License ☐ Passport

Sign Here

Sign Here

X _____

X _____

Date/Time: Ref#:

Signing Address:

Document Date	Notarization **A**ck **J**ur **O**th Fee if any	Document Description	Signer Initials	
			1	2
		Deed of Trust / Mortgage		
		Deed - General - Quit Claim - Special Warranty		
		Borrower's Title Affidavit		
		Borrower's Closing Affidavit		
		E&O / Compliance Agreement		
		Occupancy Affidavit		
		Signature Name Affidavit		
		Power of Attorney - Limited / Durable		
		T-47 Residential Real Property Affidavit		
		Mineral Rights Acknowledgement and Agreement		
		Designation of Homestead / Non-Homestead		
		Notice of Penalties for Making False or Misleading Statements		
		Ownership Affidavit		
		Occupancy and Financial Status Affidavit		
		Obligation of Debts Affidavit		
		Release of Claims and Hold Harmless Agreement		
		Affidavit of Marital Status		
		Tax Indemnity		
		Compliance / Correction Agreement		

Notes:

Ack:Do you acknowledge this as your signature and your free act and deed, for the purposes stated herein?
Jurat: Do you solemnly (swear/affirm) that this statement is true, (so help you God / on your honor)?

Signer 1 Name and Address:		Signer 2 Name and Address:	
Identification Method:☐ Personally Known ☐ Other ☐ Texas Driver's License ☐ Driver's License ☐ Passport		Identification Method:☐ Personally Known ☐ Other ☐ Texas Driver's License ☐ Driver's License ☐ Passport	
X _____		X _____	
Date/Time:		Ref#:	

Signing Address:

Document Date	Notarization **A**ck **J**ur **O**th Fee if any	Document Description	Signer Initials	
			1	2
		Deed of Trust / Mortgage		
		Deed - General - Quit Claim - Special Warranty		
		Borrower's Title Affidavit		
		Borrower's Closing Affidavit		
		E&O / Compliance Agreement		
		Occupancy Affidavit		
		Signature Name Affidavit		
		Power of Attorney - Limited / Durable		
		T-47 Residential Real Property Affidavit		
		Mineral Rights Acknowledgement and Agreement		
		Designation of Homestead / Non-Homestead		
		Notice of Penalties for Making False or Misleading Statements		
		Ownership Affidavit		
		Occupancy and Financial Status Affidavit		
		Obligation of Debts Affidavit		
		Release of Claims and Hold Harmless Agreement		
		Affidavit of Marital Status		
		Tax Indemnity		
		Compliance / Correction Agreement		

Notes:

Ack:Do you acknowledge this as your signature and your free act and deed, for the purposes stated herein?
Jurat: Do you solemnly (swear/affirm) that this statement is true, (so help you God / on your honor)?

| Signer 1 Name and Address: | | Signer 2 Name and Address: | |

| Identification Method:☐ Personally Known ☐ Other | ☐ Texas Driver's License ☐ Driver's License ☐ Passport | Identification Method:☐ Personally Known ☐ Other ☐ Texas Driver's License ☐ Driver's License ☐ Passport |

Sign Here

X _____   X _____

Date/Time: Ref#:

Signing Address:

Document Date	Notarization **Ack Jur Oth** Fee if any	Document Description	Signer Initials	
			1	2
		Deed of Trust / Mortgage		
		Deed - General - Quit Claim - Special Warranty		
		Borrower's Title Affidavit		
		Borrower's Closing Affidavit		
		E&O / Compliance Agreement		
		Occupancy Affidavit		
		Signature Name Affidavit		
		Power of Attorney - Limited / Durable		
		T-47 Residential Real Property Affidavit		
		Mineral Rights Acknowledgement and Agreement		
		Designation of Homestead / Non-Homestead		
		Notice of Penalties for Making False or Misleading Statements		
		Ownership Affidavit		
		Occupancy and Financial Status Affidavit		
		Obligation of Debts Affidavit		
		Release of Claims and Hold Harmless Agreement		
		Affidavit of Marital Status		
		Tax Indemnity		
		Compliance / Correction Agreement		

Notes:

Ack:Do you acknowledge this as your signature and your free act and deed, for the purposes stated herein?
Jurat: Do you solemnly (swear/affirm) that this statement is true, (so help you God / on your honor)?

Signer 1 Name and Address:			Signer 2 Name and Address:		

Identification Method: ☐ Personally Known ☐ Other
☐ Texas Driver's License ☐ Driver's License ☐ Passport

Identification Method: ☐ Personally Known ☐ Other
☐ Texas Driver's License ☐ Driver's License ☐ Passport

Sign Here

X _____

Sign Here

X _____

Date/Time:

Ref#:

Signing Address:

Document Date	Notarization **A**ck **J**ur **O**th Fee if any	Document Description	Signer Initials	
			1	2
		Deed of Trust / Mortgage		
		Deed - General - Quit Claim - Special Warranty		
		Borrower's Title Affidavit		
		Borrower's Closing Affidavit		
		E&O / Compliance Agreement		
		Occupancy Affidavit		
		Signature Name Affidavit		
		Power of Attorney - Limited / Durable		
		T-47 Residential Real Property Affidavit		
		Mineral Rights Acknowledgement and Agreement		
		Designation of Homestead / Non-Homestead		
		Notice of Penalties for Making False or Misleading Statements		
		Ownership Affidavit		
		Occupancy and Financial Status Affidavit		
		Obligation of Debts Affidavit		
		Release of Claims and Hold Harmless Agreement		
		Affidavit of Marital Status		
		Tax Indemnity		
		Compliance / Correction Agreement		

Notes:

Ack:Do you acknowledge this as your signature and your free act and deed, for the purposes stated herein?
Jurat: Do you solemnly (swear/affirm) that this statement is true, (so help you God / on your honor)?

Signer 1 Name and Address:		Signer 2 Name and Address:	

Identification Method:☐ Personally Known ☐ Other
☐ Texas Driver's License ☐ Driver's License ☐ Passport

Identification Method:☐ Personally Known ☐ Other
☐ Texas Driver's License ☐ Driver's License ☐ Passport

Sign Here

X _____

Sign Here

X _____

Date/Time: Ref#:

Signing Address:

Document Date	Notarization **A**ck **J**ur **O**th Fee if any	Document Description	Signer Initials	
			1	2
		Deed of Trust / Mortgage		
		Deed - General - Quit Claim - Special Warranty		
		Borrower's Title Affidavit		
		Borrower's Closing Affidavit		
		E&O / Compliance Agreement		
		Occupancy Affidavit		
		Signature Name Affidavit		
		Power of Attorney - Limited / Durable		
		T-47 Residential Real Property Affidavit		
		Mineral Rights Acknowledgement and Agreement		
		Designation of Homestead / Non-Homestead		
		Notice of Penalties for Making False or Misleading Statements		
		Ownership Affidavit		
		Occupancy and Financial Status Affidavit		
		Obligation of Debts Affidavit		
		Release of Claims and Hold Harmless Agreement		
		Affidavit of Marital Status		
		Tax Indemnity		
		Compliance / Correction Agreement		

Notes:

Ack: Do you acknowledge this as your signature and your free act and deed, for the purposes stated herein?
Jurat: Do you solemnly (swear/affirm) that this statement is true, (so help you God / on your honor)?

Signer 1 Name and Address:			Signer 2 Name and Address:		

Identification Method:☐ Personally Known ☐ Other
☐ Texas Driver's License ☐ Driver's License ☐ Passport

Identification Method:☐ Personally Known ☐ Other
☐ Texas Driver's License ☐ Driver's License ☐ Passport

Sign Here   Sign Here

X _____   X _____

Date/Time: Ref#:

Signing Address:

Document Date	Notarization **A**ck **J**ur **O**th Fee if any	Document Description	Signer Initials	
			1	2
		Deed of Trust / Mortgage		
		Deed - General - Quit Claim - Special Warranty		
		Borrower's Title Affidavit		
		Borrower's Closing Affidavit		
		E&O / Compliance Agreement		
		Occupancy Affidavit		
		Signature Name Affidavit		
		Power of Attorney - Limited / Durable		
		T-47 Residential Real Property Affidavit		
		Mineral Rights Acknowledgement and Agreement		
		Designation of Homestead / Non-Homestead		
		Notice of Penalties for Making False or Misleading Statements		
		Ownership Affidavit		
		Occupancy and Financial Status Affidavit		
		Obligation of Debts Affidavit		
		Release of Claims and Hold Harmless Agreement		
		Affidavit of Marital Status		
		Tax Indemnity		
		Compliance / Correction Agreement		

Notes:

Ack:Do you acknowledge this as your signature and your free act and deed, for the purposes stated herein?
Jurat: Do you solemnly (swear/affirm) that this statement is true, (so help you God / on your honor)?

Signer 1 Name and Address:		Signer 2 Name and Address:		

Identification Method:☐ Personally Known ☐ Other ☐ Texas Driver's License ☐ Driver's License ☐ Passport

Identification Method:☐ Personally Known ☐ Other ☐ Texas Driver's License ☐ Driver's License ☐ Passport

Sign Here

X _____

Sign Here

X _____

Date/Time:

Ref#:

Signing Address:

Document Date	Notarization **A**ck **J**ur **O**th Fee if any	Document Description	Signer Initials	
			1	2
		Deed of Trust / Mortgage		
		Deed - General - Quit Claim - Special Warranty		
		Borrower's Title Affidavit		
		Borrower's Closing Affidavit		
		E&O / Compliance Agreement		
		Occupancy Affidavit		
		Signature Name Affidavit		
		Power of Attorney - Limited / Durable		
		T-47 Residential Real Property Affidavit		
		Mineral Rights Acknowledgement and Agreement		
		Designation of Homestead / Non-Homestead		
		Notice of Penalties for Making False or Misleading Statements		
		Ownership Affidavit		
		Occupancy and Financial Status Affidavit		
		Obligation of Debts Affidavit		
		Release of Claims and Hold Harmless Agreement		
		Affidavit of Marital Status		
		Tax Indemnity		
		Compliance / Correction Agreement		

Notes:

Ack:Do you acknowledge this as your signature and your free act and deed, for the purposes stated herein?
Jurat: Do you solemnly (swear/affirm) that this statement is true, (so help you God / on your honor)?

Signer 1 Name and Address:		Signer 2 Name and Address:	

Identification Method:☐ Personally Known ☐ Other ☐ Texas Driver's License ☐ Driver's License ☐ Passport	Identification Method:☐ Personally Known ☐ Other ☐ Texas Driver's License ☐ Driver's License ☐ Passport
X _____	X _____

Date/Time:	Ref#:

Signing Address:

Document Date	Notarization **Ack Jur Oth** Fee if any	Document Description	Signer Initials	
			1	2
		Deed of Trust / Mortgage		
		Deed - General - Quit Claim - Special Warranty		
		Borrower's Title Affidavit		
		Borrower's Closing Affidavit		
		E&O / Compliance Agreement		
		Occupancy Affidavit		
		Signature Name Affidavit		
		Power of Attorney - Limited / Durable		
		T-47 Residential Real Property Affidavit		
		Mineral Rights Acknowledgement and Agreement		
		Designation of Homestead / Non-Homestead		
		Notice of Penalties for Making False or Misleading Statements		
		Ownership Affidavit		
		Occupancy and Financial Status Affidavit		
		Obligation of Debts Affidavit		
		Release of Claims and Hold Harmless Agreement		
		Affidavit of Marital Status		
		Tax Indemnity		
		Compliance / Correction Agreement		

Notes:

Ack:Do you acknowledge this as your signature and your free act and deed, for the purposes stated herein?
Jurat: Do you solemnly (swear/affirm) that this statement is true, (so help you God / on your honor)?

Signer 1 Name and Address:			Signer 2 Name and Address:		

Identification Method:☐ Personally Known ☐ Other
☐ Texas Driver's License ☐ Driver's License ☐ Passport

Identification Method:☐ Personally Known ☐ Other
☐ Texas Driver's License ☐ Driver's License ☐ Passport

Sign Here

X _____

Sign Here

X _____

Date/Time: Ref#:

Signing Address:

Document Date	Notarization **A**ck Jur **O**th Fee if any	Document Description	Signer Initials	
			1	2
		Deed of Trust / Mortgage		
		Deed - General - Quit Claim - Special Warranty		
		Borrower's Title Affidavit		
		Borrower's Closing Affidavit		
		E&O / Compliance Agreement		
		Occupancy Affidavit		
		Signature Name Affidavit		
		Power of Attorney - Limited / Durable		
		T-47 Residential Real Property Affidavit		
		Mineral Rights Acknowledgement and Agreement		
		Designation of Homestead / Non-Homestead		
		Notice of Penalties for Making False or Misleading Statements		
		Ownership Affidavit		
		Occupancy and Financial Status Affidavit		
		Obligation of Debts Affidavit		
		Release of Claims and Hold Harmless Agreement		
		Affidavit of Marital Status		
		Tax Indemnity		
		Compliance / Correction Agreement		

Notes:

Ack:Do you acknowledge this as your signature and your free act and deed, for the purposes stated herein?
Jurat: Do you solemnly (swear/affirm) that this statement is true, (so help you God / on your honor)?

Signer 1 Name and Address:			Signer 2 Name and Address:		
Identification Method:☐ Personally Known ☐ Other ☐ Texas Driver's License ☐ Driver's License ☐ Passport			Identification Method:☐ Personally Known ☐ Other ☐ Texas Driver's License ☐ Driver's License ☐ Passport		
Sign Here X _____			Sign Here X _____		
Date/Time:			Ref#:		
Signing Address:					

Document Date	Notarization **A**ck **J**ur **O**th Fee if any	Document Description	Signer Initials	
			1	2
		Deed of Trust / Mortgage		
		Deed - General - Quit Claim - Special Warranty		
		Borrower's Title Affidavit		
		Borrower's Closing Affidavit		
		E&O / Compliance Agreement		
		Occupancy Affidavit		
		Signature Name Affidavit		
		Power of Attorney - Limited / Durable		
		T-47 Residential Real Property Affidavit		
		Mineral Rights Acknowledgement and Agreement		
		Designation of Homestead / Non-Homestead		
		Notice of Penalties for Making False or Misleading Statements		
		Ownership Affidavit		
		Occupancy and Financial Status Affidavit		
		Obligation of Debts Affidavit		
		Release of Claims and Hold Harmless Agreement		
		Affidavit of Marital Status		
		Tax Indemnity		
		Compliance / Correction Agreement		

Notes:

Ack:Do you acknowledge this as your signature and your free act and deed, for the purposes stated herein?
Jurat: Do you solemnly (swear/affirm) that this statement is true, (so help you God / on your honor)?

Signer 1 Name and Address:	Signer 2 Name and Address:

Identification Method:☐ Personally Known ☐ Other
☐ Texas Driver's License ☐ Driver's License ☐ Passport

Identification Method:☐ Personally Known ☐ Other
☐ Texas Driver's License ☐ Driver's License ☐ Passport

X _____   X _____

Date/Time: Ref#:

Signing Address:

Document Date	Notarization **A**ck **J**ur **O**th Fee if any	Document Description	Signer Initials	
			1	2
		Deed of Trust / Mortgage		
		Deed - General - Quit Claim - Special Warranty		
		Borrower's Title Affidavit		
		Borrower's Closing Affidavit		
		E&O / Compliance Agreement		
		Occupancy Affidavit		
		Signature Name Affidavit		
		Power of Attorney - Limited / Durable		
		T-47 Residential Real Property Affidavit		
		Mineral Rights Acknowledgement and Agreement		
		Designation of Homestead / Non-Homestead		
		Notice of Penalties for Making False or Misleading Statements		
		Ownership Affidavit		
		Occupancy and Financial Status Affidavit		
		Obligation of Debts Affidavit		
		Release of Claims and Hold Harmless Agreement		
		Affidavit of Marital Status		
		Tax Indemnity		
		Compliance / Correction Agreement		

Notes:

Ack:Do you acknowledge this as your signature and your free act and deed, for the purposes stated herein?
Jurat: Do you solemnly (swear/affirm) that this statement is true, (so help you God / on your honor)?

Signer 1 Name and Address:		Signer 2 Name and Address:	

Identification Method:☐ Personally Known ☐ Other ☐ Texas Driver's License ☐ Driver's License ☐ Passport	Identification Method:☐ Personally Known ☐ Other ☐ Texas Driver's License ☐ Driver's License ☐ Passport

Sign Here

Sign Here

X _____   X _____

Date/Time: **Ref#:**

Signing Address:

Document Date	Notarization **A**ck **J**ur **O**th Fee if any	Document Description	Signer Initials	
			1	2
		Deed of Trust / Mortgage		
		Deed - General - Quit Claim - Special Warranty		
		Borrower's Title Affidavit		
		Borrower's Closing Affidavit		
		E&O / Compliance Agreement		
		Occupancy Affidavit		
		Signature Name Affidavit		
		Power of Attorney - Limited / Durable		
		T-47 Residential Real Property Affidavit		
		Mineral Rights Acknowledgement and Agreement		
		Designation of Homestead / Non-Homestead		
		Notice of Penalties for Making False or Misleading Statements		
		Ownership Affidavit		
		Occupancy and Financial Status Affidavit		
		Obligation of Debts Affidavit		
		Release of Claims and Hold Harmless Agreement		
		Affidavit of Marital Status		
		Tax Indemnity		
		Compliance / Correction Agreement		

Notes:

Ack:Do you acknowledge this as your signature and your free act and deed, for the purposes stated herein?
Jurat: Do you solemnly (swear/affirm) that this statement is true, (so help you God / on your honor)?

Signer 1 Name and Address:			Signer 2 Name and Address:		

Identification Method:☐ Personally Known ☐ Other
☐ Texas Driver's License ☐ Driver's License ☐ Passport

Identification Method:☐ Personally Known ☐ Other
☐ Texas Driver's License ☐ Driver's License ☐ Passport

Sign Here

Sign Here

X _____

X _____

Date/Time:

Ref#:

Signing Address:

Document Date	Notarization **A**ck **J**ur **O**th Fee if any	Document Description	Signer Initials	
			1	2
		Deed of Trust / Mortgage		
		Deed - General - Quit Claim - Special Warranty		
		Borrower's Title Affidavit		
		Borrower's Closing Affidavit		
		E&O / Compliance Agreement		
		Occupancy Affidavit		
		Signature Name Affidavit		
		Power of Attorney - Limited / Durable		
		T-47 Residential Real Property Affidavit		
		Mineral Rights Acknowledgement and Agreement		
		Designation of Homestead / Non-Homestead		
		Notice of Penalties for Making False or Misleading Statements		
		Ownership Affidavit		
		Occupancy and Financial Status Affidavit		
		Obligation of Debts Affidavit		
		Release of Claims and Hold Harmless Agreement		
		Affidavit of Marital Status		
		Tax Indemnity		
		Compliance / Correction Agreement		

Notes:

Ack:Do you acknowledge this as your signature and your free act and deed, for the purposes stated herein?
Jurat: Do you solemnly (swear/affirm) that this statement is true, (so help you God / on your honor)?

Signer 1 Name and Address:		Signer 2 Name and Address:	

Identification Method:☐ Personally Known ☐ Other
☐ Texas Driver's License ☐ Driver's License ☐ Passport

Identification Method:☐ Personally Known ☐ Other
☐ Texas Driver's License ☐ Driver's License ☐ Passport

Sign Here

X _____

Sign Here

X _____

Date/Time: Ref#:

Signing Address:

Document Date	Notarization **A**ck **J**ur **O**th Fee if any	Document Description	Signer Initials	
			1	2
		Deed of Trust / Mortgage		
		Deed - General - Quit Claim - Special Warranty		
		Borrower's Title Affidavit		
		Borrower's Closing Affidavit		
		E&O / Compliance Agreement		
		Occupancy Affidavit		
		Signature Name Affidavit		
		Power of Attorney - Limited / Durable		
		T-47 Residential Real Property Affidavit		
		Mineral Rights Acknowledgement and Agreement		
		Designation of Homestead / Non-Homestead		
		Notice of Penalties for Making False or Misleading Statements		
		Ownership Affidavit		
		Occupancy and Financial Status Affidavit		
		Obligation of Debts Affidavit		
		Release of Claims and Hold Harmless Agreement		
		Affidavit of Marital Status		
		Tax Indemnity		
		Compliance / Correction Agreement		

Notes:

Ack:Do you acknowledge this as your signature and your free act and deed, for the purposes stated herein?
Jurat: Do you solemnly (swear/affirm) that this statement is true, (so help you God / on your honor)?

Signer 1 Name and Address:			Signer 2 Name and Address:		

Identification Method:☐ Personally Known ☐ Other
☐ Texas Driver's License ☐ Driver's License ☐ Passport

Identification Method:☐ Personally Known ☐ Other
☐ Texas Driver's License ☐ Driver's License ☐ Passport

Sign Here

X _____

Sign Here

X _____

Date/Time: Ref#:

Signing Address:

Document Date	Notarization **A**ck **J**ur **O**th Fee if any	Document Description	Signer Initials	
			1	2
		Deed of Trust / Mortgage		
		Deed - General - Quit Claim - Special Warranty		
		Borrower's Title Affidavit		
		Borrower's Closing Affidavit		
		E&O / Compliance Agreement		
		Occupancy Affidavit		
		Signature Name Affidavit		
		Power of Attorney - Limited / Durable		
		T-47 Residential Real Property Affidavit		
		Mineral Rights Acknowledgement and Agreement		
		Designation of Homestead / Non-Homestead		
		Notice of Penalties for Making False or Misleading Statements		
		Ownership Affidavit		
		Occupancy and Financial Status Affidavit		
		Obligation of Debts Affidavit		
		Release of Claims and Hold Harmless Agreement		
		Affidavit of Marital Status		
		Tax Indemnity		
		Compliance / Correction Agreement		

Notes:

Ack:Do you acknowledge this as your signature and your free act and deed, for the purposes stated herein?
Jurat: Do you solemnly (swear/affirm) that this statement is true, (so help you God / on your honor)?

Signer 1 Name and Address:		Signer 2 Name and Address:	
Identification Method:☐ Personally Known ☐ Other ☐ Texas Driver's License ☐ Driver's License ☐ Passport		Identification Method:☐ Personally Known ☐ Other ☐ Texas Driver's License ☐ Driver's License ☐ Passport	
Sign Here X _____		Sign Here X _____	
Date/Time:		Ref#:	
Signing Address:			

Document Date	Notarization **A**ck **J**ur **O**th Fee if any	Document Description	Signer Initials	
			1	2
		Deed of Trust / Mortgage		
		Deed - General - Quit Claim - Special Warranty		
		Borrower's Title Affidavit		
		Borrower's Closing Affidavit		
		E&O / Compliance Agreement		
		Occupancy Affidavit		
		Signature Name Affidavit		
		Power of Attorney - Limited / Durable		
		T-47 Residential Real Property Affidavit		
		Mineral Rights Acknowledgement and Agreement		
		Designation of Homestead / Non-Homestead		
		Notice of Penalties for Making False or Misleading Statements		
		Ownership Affidavit		
		Occupancy and Financial Status Affidavit		
		Obligation of Debts Affidavit		
		Release of Claims and Hold Harmless Agreement		
		Affidavit of Marital Status		
		Tax Indemnity		
		Compliance / Correction Agreement		

Notes:

Ack: Do you acknowledge this as your signature and your free act and deed, for the purposes stated herein?
Jurat: Do you solemnly (swear/affirm) that this statement is true, (so help you God / on your honor)?

Signer 1 Name and Address:		Signer 2 Name and Address:	

Identification Method:☐ Personally Known ☐ Other
☐ Texas Driver's License ☐ Driver's License ☐ Passport

Identification Method:☐ Personally Known ☐ Other
☐ Texas Driver's License ☐ Driver's License ☐ Passport

Sign Here

Sign Here

X _____

X _____

Date/Time: Ref#:

Signing Address:

Document Date	Notarization **A**ck **J**ur **O**th Fee if any	Document Description	Signer Initials	
			1	2
		Deed of Trust / Mortgage		
		Deed - General - Quit Claim - Special Warranty		
		Borrower's Title Affidavit		
		Borrower's Closing Affidavit		
		E&O / Compliance Agreement		
		Occupancy Affidavit		
		Signature Name Affidavit		
		Power of Attorney - Limited / Durable		
		T-47 Residential Real Property Affidavit		
		Mineral Rights Acknowledgement and Agreement		
		Designation of Homestead / Non-Homestead		
		Notice of Penalties for Making False or Misleading Statements		
		Ownership Affidavit		
		Occupancy and Financial Status Affidavit		
		Obligation of Debts Affidavit		
		Release of Claims and Hold Harmless Agreement		
		Affidavit of Marital Status		
		Tax Indemnity		
		Compliance / Correction Agreement		

Notes:

Ack:Do you acknowledge this as your signature and your free act and deed, for the purposes stated herein?
Jurat: Do you solemnly (swear/affirm) that this statement is true, (so help you God / on your honor)?

Signer 1 Name and Address:			Signer 2 Name and Address:		

Identification Method:☐ Personally Known ☐ Other
☐ Texas Driver's License ☐ Driver's License ☐ Passport

Identification Method:☐ Personally Known ☐ Other
☐ Texas Driver's License ☐ Driver's License ☐ Passport

Sign Here

X _____

Sign Here

X _____

Date/Time: **Ref#:**

Signing Address:

Document Date	Notarization **A**ck **J**ur **O**th Fee if any	Document Description	Signer Initials	
			1	2
		Deed of Trust / Mortgage		
		Deed - General - Quit Claim - Special Warranty		
		Borrower's Title Affidavit		
		Borrower's Closing Affidavit		
		E&O / Compliance Agreement		
		Occupancy Affidavit		
		Signature Name Affidavit		
		Power of Attorney - Limited / Durable		
		T-47 Residential Real Property Affidavit		
		Mineral Rights Acknowledgement and Agreement		
		Designation of Homestead / Non-Homestead		
		Notice of Penalties for Making False or Misleading Statements		
		Ownership Affidavit		
		Occupancy and Financial Status Affidavit		
		Obligation of Debts Affidavit		
		Release of Claims and Hold Harmless Agreement		
		Affidavit of Marital Status		
		Tax Indemnity		
		Compliance / Correction Agreement		

Notes:

Ack:Do you acknowledge this as your signature and your free act and deed, for the purposes stated herein?
Jurat: Do you solemnly (swear/affirm) that this statement is true, (so help you God / on your honor)?
64

Signer 1 Name and Address:							Signer 2 Name and Address:		

Identification Method: ☐ Personally Known ☐ Other
☐ Texas Driver's License ☐ Driver's License ☐ Passport

Identification Method: ☐ Personally Known ☐ Other
☐ Texas Driver's License ☐ Driver's License ☐ Passport

Sign Here

Sign Here

X _____

X _____

Date/Time:

Ref#:

Signing Address:

Document Date	Notarization **A**ck Jur **O**th Fee if any	Document Description	Signer Initials	
			1	2
		Deed of Trust / Mortgage		
		Deed - General - Quit Claim - Special Warranty		
		Borrower's Title Affidavit		
		Borrower's Closing Affidavit		
		E&O / Compliance Agreement		
		Occupancy Affidavit		
		Signature Name Affidavit		
		Power of Attorney - Limited / Durable		
		T-47 Residential Real Property Affidavit		
		Mineral Rights Acknowledgement and Agreement		
		Designation of Homestead / Non-Homestead		
		Notice of Penalties for Making False or Misleading Statements		
		Ownership Affidavit		
		Occupancy and Financial Status Affidavit		
		Obligation of Debts Affidavit		
		Release of Claims and Hold Harmless Agreement		
		Affidavit of Marital Status		
		Tax Indemnity		
		Compliance / Correction Agreement		

Notes:

Ack: Do you acknowledge this as your signature and your free act and deed, for the purposes stated herein?
Jurat: Do you solemnly (swear/affirm) that this statement is true, (so help you God / on your honor)?

Signer 1 Name and Address:			Signer 2 Name and Address:		

Identification Method: ☐ Personally Known ☐ Other
☐ Texas Driver's License ☐ Driver's License ☐ Passport

Identification Method: ☐ Personally Known ☐ Other
☐ Texas Driver's License ☐ Driver's License ☐ Passport

Sign Here

Sign Here

X _____ X _____

Date/Time: Ref#:

Signing Address:

Document Date	Notarization **A**ck **J**ur **O**th Fee if any	Document Description	Signer Initials	
			1	2
		Deed of Trust / Mortgage		
		Deed - General - Quit Claim - Special Warranty		
		Borrower's Title Affidavit		
		Borrower's Closing Affidavit		
		E&O / Compliance Agreement		
		Occupancy Affidavit		
		Signature Name Affidavit		
		Power of Attorney - Limited / Durable		
		T-47 Residential Real Property Affidavit		
		Mineral Rights Acknowledgement and Agreement		
		Designation of Homestead / Non-Homestead		
		Notice of Penalties for Making False or Misleading Statements		
		Ownership Affidavit		
		Occupancy and Financial Status Affidavit		
		Obligation of Debts Affidavit		
		Release of Claims and Hold Harmless Agreement		
		Affidavit of Marital Status		
		Tax Indemnity		
		Compliance / Correction Agreement		

Notes:

Ack:Do you acknowledge this as your signature and your free act and deed, for the purposes stated herein?
Jurat: Do you solemnly (swear/affirm) that this statement is true, (so help you God / on your honor)?

66

Signer 1 Name and Address:		Signer 2 Name and Address:	

Identification Method:☐ Personally Known ☐ Other
☐ Texas Driver's License ☐ Driver's License ☐ Passport

Identification Method:☐ Personally Known ☐ Other
☐ Texas Driver's License ☐ Driver's License ☐ Passport

Sign Here

X _____

Sign Here

X _____

Date/Time: Ref#:

Signing Address:

Document Date	Notarization **Ack Jur Oth** Fee if any	Document Description	Signer Initials	
			1	2
		Deed of Trust / Mortgage		
		Deed - General - Quit Claim - Special Warranty		
		Borrower's Title Affidavit		
		Borrower's Closing Affidavit		
		E&O / Compliance Agreement		
		Occupancy Affidavit		
		Signature Name Affidavit		
		Power of Attorney - Limited / Durable		
		T-47 Residential Real Property Affidavit		
		Mineral Rights Acknowledgement and Agreement		
		Designation of Homestead / Non-Homestead		
		Notice of Penalties for Making False or Misleading Statements		
		Ownership Affidavit		
		Occupancy and Financial Status Affidavit		
		Obligation of Debts Affidavit		
		Release of Claims and Hold Harmless Agreement		
		Affidavit of Marital Status		
		Tax Indemnity		
		Compliance / Correction Agreement		

Notes:

Ack:Do you acknowledge this as your signature and your free act and deed, for the purposes stated herein?
Jurat: Do you solemnly (swear/affirm) that this statement is true, (so help you God / on your honor)?

Signer 1 Name and Address:		Signer 2 Name and Address:	
Identification Method:☐ Personally Known ☐ Other ☐ Texas Driver's License ☐ Driver's License ☐ Passport		Identification Method:☐ Personally Known ☐ Other ☐ Texas Driver's License ☐ Driver's License ☐ Passport	
Sign Here X _____		Sign Here X _____	
Date/Time:		Ref#:	
Signing Address:			

Document Date	Notarization **A**ck **J**ur **O**th Fee if any	Document Description	Signer Initials	
			1	2
		Deed of Trust / Mortgage		
		Deed - General - Quit Claim - Special Warranty		
		Borrower's Title Affidavit		
		Borrower's Closing Affidavit		
		E&O / Compliance Agreement		
		Occupancy Affidavit		
		Signature Name Affidavit		
		Power of Attorney - Limited / Durable		
		T-47 Residential Real Property Affidavit		
		Mineral Rights Acknowledgement and Agreement		
		Designation of Homestead / Non-Homestead		
		Notice of Penalties for Making False or Misleading Statements		
		Ownership Affidavit		
		Occupancy and Financial Status Affidavit		
		Obligation of Debts Affidavit		
		Release of Claims and Hold Harmless Agreement		
		Affidavit of Marital Status		
		Tax Indemnity		
		Compliance / Correction Agreement		

Notes:

Ack:Do you acknowledge this as your signature and your free act and deed, for the purposes stated herein?
Jurat: Do you solemnly (swear/affirm) that this statement is true, (so help you God / on your honor)?

Signer 1 Name and Address:		Signer 2 Name and Address:	

Identification Method:☐ Personally Known ☐ Other
☐ Texas Driver's License ☐ Driver's License ☐ Passport

Identification Method:☐ Personally Known ☐ Other
☐ Texas Driver's License ☐ Driver's License ☐ Passport

Sign Here

X _____

Sign Here

X _____

Date/Time: Ref#:

Signing Address:

Document Date	Notarization **A**ck **J**ur **O**th Fee if any	Document Description	Signer Initials	
			1	2
		Deed of Trust / Mortgage		
		Deed - General - Quit Claim - Special Warranty		
		Borrower's Title Affidavit		
		Borrower's Closing Affidavit		
		E&O / Compliance Agreement		
		Occupancy Affidavit		
		Signature Name Affidavit		
		Power of Attorney - Limited / Durable		
		T-47 Residential Real Property Affidavit		
		Mineral Rights Acknowledgement and Agreement		
		Designation of Homestead / Non-Homestead		
		Notice of Penalties for Making False or Misleading Statements		
		Ownership Affidavit		
		Occupancy and Financial Status Affidavit		
		Obligation of Debts Affidavit		
		Release of Claims and Hold Harmless Agreement		
		Affidavit of Marital Status		
		Tax Indemnity		
		Compliance / Correction Agreement		

Notes:

Ack:Do you acknowledge this as your signature and your free act and deed, for the purposes stated herein?
Jurat: Do you solemnly (swear/affirm) that this statement is true, (so help you God / on your honor)?

Signer 1 Name and Address:		Signer 2 Name and Address:			

Identification Method: ☐ Personally Known ☐ Other
☐ Texas Driver's License ☐ Driver's License ☐ Passport

Identification Method: ☐ Personally Known ☐ Other
☐ Texas Driver's License ☐ Driver's License ☐ Passport

Sign Here

Sign Here

X _____   X _____

Date/Time: Ref#:

Signing Address:

Document Date	Notarization **A**ck **J**ur **O**th Fee if any	Document Description	Signer Initials	
			1	2
		Deed of Trust / Mortgage		
		Deed - General - Quit Claim - Special Warranty		
		Borrower's Title Affidavit		
		Borrower's Closing Affidavit		
		E&O / Compliance Agreement		
		Occupancy Affidavit		
		Signature Name Affidavit		
		Power of Attorney - Limited / Durable		
		T-47 Residential Real Property Affidavit		
		Mineral Rights Acknowledgement and Agreement		
		Designation of Homestead / Non-Homestead		
		Notice of Penalties for Making False or Misleading Statements		
		Ownership Affidavit		
		Occupancy and Financial Status Affidavit		
		Obligation of Debts Affidavit		
		Release of Claims and Hold Harmless Agreement		
		Affidavit of Marital Status		
		Tax Indemnity		
		Compliance / Correction Agreement		

Notes:

Ack: Do you acknowledge this as your signature and your free act and deed, for the purposes stated herein?
Jurat: Do you solemnly (swear/affirm) that this statement is true, (so help you God / on your honor)?

Signer 1 Name and Address:			Signer 2 Name and Address:		

Identification Method:☐ Personally Known ☐ Other
☐ Texas Driver's License ☐ Driver's License ☐ Passport

Identification Method:☐ Personally Known ☐ Other
☐ Texas Driver's License ☐ Driver's License ☐ Passport

Sign Here

Sign Here

X _____

X _____

Date/Time: _____ Ref#: _____

Signing Address:

Document Date	Notarization **A**ck **J**ur **O**th Fee if any	Document Description	Signer Initials	
			1	2
		Deed of Trust / Mortgage		
		Deed - General - Quit Claim - Special Warranty		
		Borrower's Title Affidavit		
		Borrower's Closing Affidavit		
		E&O / Compliance Agreement		
		Occupancy Affidavit		
		Signature Name Affidavit		
		Power of Attorney - Limited / Durable		
		T-47 Residential Real Property Affidavit		
		Mineral Rights Acknowledgement and Agreement		
		Designation of Homestead / Non-Homestead		
		Notice of Penalties for Making False or Misleading Statements		
		Ownership Affidavit		
		Occupancy and Financial Status Affidavit		
		Obligation of Debts Affidavit		
		Release of Claims and Hold Harmless Agreement		
		Affidavit of Marital Status		
		Tax Indemnity		
		Compliance / Correction Agreement		

Notes:

Ack:Do you acknowledge this as your signature and your free act and deed, for the purposes stated herein?
Jurat: Do you solemnly (swear/affirm) that this statement is true, (so help you God / on your honor)?

Signer 1 Name and Address:		Signer 2 Name and Address:	
Identification Method: ☐ Personally Known ☐ Other ☐ Texas Driver's License ☐ Driver's License ☐ Passport		Identification Method: ☐ Personally Known ☐ Other ☐ Texas Driver's License ☐ Driver's License ☐ Passport	
Sign Here X _____		Sign Here X _____	
Date/Time:		Ref#:	

Signing Address:

Document Date	Notarization **A**ck **J**ur **O**th Fee if any	Document Description	Signer Initials	
			1	2
		Deed of Trust / Mortgage		
		Deed - General - Quit Claim - Special Warranty		
		Borrower's Title Affidavit		
		Borrower's Closing Affidavit		
		E&O / Compliance Agreement		
		Occupancy Affidavit		
		Signature Name Affidavit		
		Power of Attorney - Limited / Durable		
		T-47 Residential Real Property Affidavit		
		Mineral Rights Acknowledgement and Agreement		
		Designation of Homestead / Non-Homestead		
		Notice of Penalties for Making False or Misleading Statements		
		Ownership Affidavit		
		Occupancy and Financial Status Affidavit		
		Obligation of Debts Affidavit		
		Release of Claims and Hold Harmless Agreement		
		Affidavit of Marital Status		
		Tax Indemnity		
		Compliance / Correction Agreement		

Notes:

Ack:Do you acknowledge this as your signature and your free act and deed, for the purposes stated herein?
Jurat: Do you solemnly (swear/affirm) that this statement is true, (so help you God / on your honor)?

Signer 1 Name and Address:		Signer 2 Name and Address:	

Identification Method:☐ Personally Known ☐ Other ☐ Texas Driver's License ☐ Driver's License ☐ Passport	Identification Method:☐ Personally Known ☐ Other ☐ Texas Driver's License ☐ Driver's License ☐ Passport
Sign Here X _____	Sign Here X _____

Date/Time: Ref#:

Signing Address:

Document Date	Notarization **A**ck **J**ur **O**th Fee if any	Document Description	Signer Initials	
			1	2
		Deed of Trust / Mortgage		
		Deed - General - Quit Claim - Special Warranty		
		Borrower's Title Affidavit		
		Borrower's Closing Affidavit		
		E&O / Compliance Agreement		
		Occupancy Affidavit		
		Signature Name Affidavit		
		Power of Attorney - Limited / Durable		
		T-47 Residential Real Property Affidavit		
		Mineral Rights Acknowledgement and Agreement		
		Designation of Homestead / Non-Homestead		
		Notice of Penalties for Making False or Misleading Statements		
		Ownership Affidavit		
		Occupancy and Financial Status Affidavit		
		Obligation of Debts Affidavit		
		Release of Claims and Hold Harmless Agreement		
		Affidavit of Marital Status		
		Tax Indemnity		
		Compliance / Correction Agreement		

Notes:

Ack:Do you acknowledge this as your signature and your free act and deed, for the purposes stated herein?
Jurat: Do you solemnly (swear/affirm) that this statement is true, (so help you God / on your honor)?

Signer 1 Name and Address:		Signer 2 Name and Address:	
Identification Method:☐ Personally Known ☐ Other ☐ Texas Driver's License ☐ Driver's License ☐ Passport		Identification Method:☐ Personally Known ☐ Other ☐ Texas Driver's License ☐ Driver's License ☐ Passport	
Sign Here		Sign Here	
X _____		X _____	
Date/Time:		Ref#:	

Signing Address:

Document Date	Notarization **A**ck **J**ur **O**th Fee if any	Document Description	Signer Initials	
			1	2
		Deed of Trust / Mortgage		
		Deed - General - Quit Claim - Special Warranty		
		Borrower's Title Affidavit		
		Borrower's Closing Affidavit		
		E&O / Compliance Agreement		
		Occupancy Affidavit		
		Signature Name Affidavit		
		Power of Attorney - Limited / Durable		
		T-47 Residential Real Property Affidavit		
		Mineral Rights Acknowledgement and Agreement		
		Designation of Homestead / Non-Homestead		
		Notice of Penalties for Making False or Misleading Statements		
		Ownership Affidavit		
		Occupancy and Financial Status Affidavit		
		Obligation of Debts Affidavit		
		Release of Claims and Hold Harmless Agreement		
		Affidavit of Marital Status		
		Tax Indemnity		
		Compliance / Correction Agreement		

Notes:

Ack: Do you acknowledge this as your signature and your free act and deed, for the purposes stated herein?
Jurat: Do you solemnly (swear/affirm) that this statement is true, (so help you God / on your honor)?

Signer 1 Name and Address:		Signer 2 Name and Address:	

Identification Method:☐ Personally Known ☐ Other ☐ Texas Driver's License ☐ Driver's License ☐ Passport	Identification Method:☐ Personally Known ☐ Other ☐ Texas Driver's License ☐ Driver's License ☐ Passport

Sign Here   Sign Here

X _____   X _____

Date/Time: **Ref#:**

Signing Address:

Document Date	Notarization **A**ck Jur **O**th Fee if any	Document Description	Signer Initials	
			1	2
		Deed of Trust / Mortgage		
		Deed - General - Quit Claim - Special Warranty		
		Borrower's Title Affidavit		
		Borrower's Closing Affidavit		
		E&O / Compliance Agreement		
		Occupancy Affidavit		
		Signature Name Affidavit		
		Power of Attorney - Limited / Durable		
		T-47 Residential Real Property Affidavit		
		Mineral Rights Acknowledgement and Agreement		
		Designation of Homestead / Non-Homestead		
		Notice of Penalties for Making False or Misleading Statements		
		Ownership Affidavit		
		Occupancy and Financial Status Affidavit		
		Obligation of Debts Affidavit		
		Release of Claims and Hold Harmless Agreement		
		Affidavit of Marital Status		
		Tax Indemnity		
		Compliance / Correction Agreement		

Notes:

Ack: Do you acknowledge this as your signature and your free act and deed, for the purposes stated herein?
Jurat: Do you solemnly (swear/affirm) that this statement is true, (so help you God / on your honor)?

Signer 1 Name and Address:		Signer 2 Name and Address:	
Identification Method:☐ Personally Known ☐ Other ☐ Texas Driver's License ☐ Driver's License ☐ Passport		Identification Method:☐ Personally Known ☐ Other ☐ Texas Driver's License ☐ Driver's License ☐ Passport	
Sign Here		Sign Here	
X _____		X _____	
Date/Time:		Ref#:	

Signing Address:

Document Date	Notarization **A**ck **J**ur **O**th Fee if any	Document Description	Signer Initials	
			1	2
		Deed of Trust / Mortgage		
		Deed - General - Quit Claim - Special Warranty		
		Borrower's Title Affidavit		
		Borrower's Closing Affidavit		
		E&O / Compliance Agreement		
		Occupancy Affidavit		
		Signature Name Affidavit		
		Power of Attorney - Limited / Durable		
		T-47 Residential Real Property Affidavit		
		Mineral Rights Acknowledgement and Agreement		
		Designation of Homestead / Non-Homestead		
		Notice of Penalties for Making False or Misleading Statements		
		Ownership Affidavit		
		Occupancy and Financial Status Affidavit		
		Obligation of Debts Affidavit		
		Release of Claims and Hold Harmless Agreement		
		Affidavit of Marital Status		
		Tax Indemnity		
		Compliance / Correction Agreement		

Notes:

Ack:Do you acknowledge this as your signature and your free act and deed, for the purposes stated herein?
Jurat: Do you solemnly (swear/affirm) that this statement is true, (so help you God / on your honor)?

Signer 1 Name and Address:		Signer 2 Name and Address:	

Identification Method:☐ Personally Known ☐ Other
☐ Texas Driver's License ☐ Driver's License ☐ Passport

Identification Method:☐ Personally Known ☐ Other
☐ Texas Driver's License ☐ Driver's License ☐ Passport

Sign Here

X _____

Sign Here

X _____

Date/Time: **Ref#:**

Signing Address:

Document Date	Notarization **A**ck **Jur O**th Fee if any	Document Description	Signer Initials	
			1	2
		Deed of Trust / Mortgage		
		Deed - General - Quit Claim - Special Warranty		
		Borrower's Title Affidavit		
		Borrower's Closing Affidavit		
		E&O / Compliance Agreement		
		Occupancy Affidavit		
		Signature Name Affidavit		
		Power of Attorney - Limited / Durable		
		T-47 Residential Real Property Affidavit		
		Mineral Rights Acknowledgement and Agreement		
		Designation of Homestead / Non-Homestead		
		Notice of Penalties for Making False or Misleading Statements		
		Ownership Affidavit		
		Occupancy and Financial Status Affidavit		
		Obligation of Debts Affidavit		
		Release of Claims and Hold Harmless Agreement		
		Affidavit of Marital Status		
		Tax Indemnity		
		Compliance / Correction Agreement		

Notes:

Ack:Do you acknowledge this as your signature and your free act and deed, for the purposes stated herein?
Jurat: Do you solemnly (swear/affirm) that this statement is true, (so help you God / on your honor)?

Signer 1 Name and Address:		Signer 2 Name and Address:	
Identification Method:☐ Personally Known ☐ Other ☐ Texas Driver's License ☐ Driver's License ☐ Passport		Identification Method:☐ Personally Known ☐ Other ☐ Texas Driver's License ☐ Driver's License ☐ Passport	
Sign Here X _____		Sign Here X _____	
Date/Time:		Ref#:	

Signing Address:

Document Date	Notarization **A**ck **J**ur **O**th Fee if any	Document Description	Signer Initials	
			1	2
		Deed of Trust / Mortgage		
		Deed - General - Quit Claim - Special Warranty		
		Borrower's Title Affidavit		
		Borrower's Closing Affidavit		
		E&O / Compliance Agreement		
		Occupancy Affidavit		
		Signature Name Affidavit		
		Power of Attorney - Limited / Durable		
		T-47 Residential Real Property Affidavit		
		Mineral Rights Acknowledgement and Agreement		
		Designation of Homestead / Non-Homestead		
		Notice of Penalties for Making False or Misleading Statements		
		Ownership Affidavit		
		Occupancy and Financial Status Affidavit		
		Obligation of Debts Affidavit		
		Release of Claims and Hold Harmless Agreement		
		Affidavit of Marital Status		
		Tax Indemnity		
		Compliance / Correction Agreement		

Notes:

Ack:Do you acknowledge this as your signature and your free act and deed, for the purposes stated herein?
Jurat: Do you solemnly (swear/affirm) that this statement is true, (so help you God / on your honor)?

Signer 1 Name and Address:		Signer 2 Name and Address:	

Identification Method:☐ Personally Known ☐ Other ☐ Texas Driver's License ☐ Driver's License ☐ Passport	Identification Method:☐ Personally Known ☐ Other ☐ Texas Driver's License ☐ Driver's License ☐ Passport

Sign Here

Sign Here

X _____ X _____

Date/Time: **Ref#:**

Signing Address:

Document Date	Notarization **A**ck **J**ur **O**th Fee if any	Document Description	Signer Initials	
			1	2
		Deed of Trust / Mortgage		
		Deed - General - Quit Claim - Special Warranty		
		Borrower's Title Affidavit		
		Borrower's Closing Affidavit		
		E&O / Compliance Agreement		
		Occupancy Affidavit		
		Signature Name Affidavit		
		Power of Attorney - Limited / Durable		
		T-47 Residential Real Property Affidavit		
		Mineral Rights Acknowledgement and Agreement		
		Designation of Homestead / Non-Homestead		
		Notice of Penalties for Making False or Misleading Statements		
		Ownership Affidavit		
		Occupancy and Financial Status Affidavit		
		Obligation of Debts Affidavit		
		Release of Claims and Hold Harmless Agreement		
		Affidavit of Marital Status		
		Tax Indemnity		
		Compliance / Correction Agreement		

Notes:

Ack:Do you acknowledge this as your signature and your free act and deed, for the purposes stated herein?
Jurat: Do you solemnly (swear/affirm) that this statement is true, (so help you God / on your honor)?

Signer 1 Name and Address:			Signer 2 Name and Address:		
Identification Method:☐ Personally Known ☐ Other ☐ Texas Driver's License ☐ Driver's License ☐ Passport			Identification Method:☐ Personally Known ☐ Other ☐ Texas Driver's License ☐ Driver's License ☐ Passport		

X _____   X _____

Date/Time: Ref#:

Signing Address:

Document Date	Notarization **A**ck **J**ur **O**th Fee if any	Document Description	Signer Initials	
			1	2
		Deed of Trust / Mortgage		
		Deed - General - Quit Claim - Special Warranty		
		Borrower's Title Affidavit		
		Borrower's Closing Affidavit		
		E&O / Compliance Agreement		
		Occupancy Affidavit		
		Signature Name Affidavit		
		Power of Attorney - Limited / Durable		
		T-47 Residential Real Property Affidavit		
		Mineral Rights Acknowledgement and Agreement		
		Designation of Homestead / Non-Homestead		
		Notice of Penalties for Making False or Misleading Statements		
		Ownership Affidavit		
		Occupancy and Financial Status Affidavit		
		Obligation of Debts Affidavit		
		Release of Claims and Hold Harmless Agreement		
		Affidavit of Marital Status		
		Tax Indemnity		
		Compliance / Correction Agreement		

Notes:

Ack:Do you acknowledge this as your signature and your free act and deed, for the purposes stated herein?
Jurat: Do you solemnly (swear/affirm) that this statement is true, (so help you God / on your honor)?

Signer 1 Name and Address:			Signer 2 Name and Address:		

Identification Method:☐ Personally Known ☐ Other
☐ Texas Driver's License ☐ Driver's License ☐ Passport

Identification Method:☐ Personally Known ☐ Other
☐ Texas Driver's License ☐ Driver's License ☐ Passport

X _____

X _____

Date/Time: Ref#:

Signing Address:

Document Date	Notarization **A**ck **J**ur **O**th Fee if any	Document Description	Signer Initials	
			1	2
		Deed of Trust / Mortgage		
		Deed - General - Quit Claim - Special Warranty		
		Borrower's Title Affidavit		
		Borrower's Closing Affidavit		
		E&O / Compliance Agreement		
		Occupancy Affidavit		
		Signature Name Affidavit		
		Power of Attorney - Limited / Durable		
		T-47 Residential Real Property Affidavit		
		Mineral Rights Acknowledgement and Agreement		
		Designation of Homestead / Non-Homestead		
		Notice of Penalties for Making False or Misleading Statements		
		Ownership Affidavit		
		Occupancy and Financial Status Affidavit		
		Obligation of Debts Affidavit		
		Release of Claims and Hold Harmless Agreement		
		Affidavit of Marital Status		
		Tax Indemnity		
		Compliance / Correction Agreement		

Notes:

Ack:Do you acknowledge this as your signature and your free act and deed, for the purposes stated herein?
Jurat: Do you solemnly (swear/affirm) that this statement is true, (so help you God / on your honor)?

Signer 1 Name and Address:		Signer 2 Name and Address:	

Identification Method: ☐ Personally Known ☐ Other
☐ Texas Driver's License ☐ Driver's License ☐ Passport

Identification Method: ☐ Personally Known ☐ Other
☐ Texas Driver's License ☐ Driver's License ☐ Passport

Sign Here

Sign Here

X _____

X _____

Date/Time: Ref#:

Signing Address:

Document Date	Notarization **A**ck **J**ur **O**th Fee if any	Document Description	Signer Initials	
			1	2
		Deed of Trust / Mortgage		
		Deed - General - Quit Claim - Special Warranty		
		Borrower's Title Affidavit		
		Borrower's Closing Affidavit		
		E&O / Compliance Agreement		
		Occupancy Affidavit		
		Signature Name Affidavit		
		Power of Attorney - Limited / Durable		
		T-47 Residential Real Property Affidavit		
		Mineral Rights Acknowledgement and Agreement		
		Designation of Homestead / Non-Homestead		
		Notice of Penalties for Making False or Misleading Statements		
		Ownership Affidavit		
		Occupancy and Financial Status Affidavit		
		Obligation of Debts Affidavit		
		Release of Claims and Hold Harmless Agreement		
		Affidavit of Marital Status		
		Tax Indemnity		
		Compliance / Correction Agreement		

Notes:

Ack: Do you acknowledge this as your signature and your free act and deed, for the purposes stated herein?
Jurat: Do you solemnly (swear/affirm) that this statement is true, (so help you God / on your honor)?

Signer 1 Name and Address:		Signer 2 Name and Address:	

Identification Method:☐ Personally Known ☐ Other
☐ Texas Driver's License ☐ Driver's License ☐ Passport

Identification Method:☐ Personally Known ☐ Other
☐ Texas Driver's License ☐ Driver's License ☐ Passport

Sign Here

Sign Here

X _____

X _____

Date/Time: Ref#:

Signing Address:

Document Date	Notarization **A**ck **J**ur **O**th Fee if any	Document Description	Signer Initials	
			1	2
		Deed of Trust / Mortgage		
		Deed - General - Quit Claim - Special Warranty		
		Borrower's Title Affidavit		
		Borrower's Closing Affidavit		
		E&O / Compliance Agreement		
		Occupancy Affidavit		
		Signature Name Affidavit		
		Power of Attorney - Limited / Durable		
		T-47 Residential Real Property Affidavit		
		Mineral Rights Acknowledgement and Agreement		
		Designation of Homestead / Non-Homestead		
		Notice of Penalties for Making False or Misleading Statements		
		Ownership Affidavit		
		Occupancy and Financial Status Affidavit		
		Obligation of Debts Affidavit		
		Release of Claims and Hold Harmless Agreement		
		Affidavit of Marital Status		
		Tax Indemnity		
		Compliance / Correction Agreement		

Notes:

Ack:Do you acknowledge this as your signature and your free act and deed, for the purposes stated herein?
Jurat: Do you solemnly (swear/affirm) that this statement is true, (so help you God / on your honor)?

Signer 1 Name and Address:		Signer 2 Name and Address:	

Identification Method:☐ Personally Known ☐ Other ☐ Texas Driver's License ☐ Driver's License ☐ Passport	Identification Method:☐ Personally Known ☐ Other ☐ Texas Driver's License ☐ Driver's License ☐ Passport

Sign Here

X _____

Sign Here

X _____

Date/Time: Ref#:

Signing Address:

Document Date	Notarization **A**ck **J**ur **O**th Fee if any	Document Description	Signer Initials	
			1	2
		Deed of Trust / Mortgage		
		Deed - General - Quit Claim - Special Warranty		
		Borrower's Title Affidavit		
		Borrower's Closing Affidavit		
		E&O / Compliance Agreement		
		Occupancy Affidavit		
		Signature Name Affidavit		
		Power of Attorney - Limited / Durable		
		T-47 Residential Real Property Affidavit		
		Mineral Rights Acknowledgement and Agreement		
		Designation of Homestead / Non-Homestead		
		Notice of Penalties for Making False or Misleading Statements		
		Ownership Affidavit		
		Occupancy and Financial Status Affidavit		
		Obligation of Debts Affidavit		
		Release of Claims and Hold Harmless Agreement		
		Affidavit of Marital Status		
		Tax Indemnity		
		Compliance / Correction Agreement		

Notes:

Ack:Do you acknowledge this as your signature and your free act and deed, for the purposes stated herein?
Jurat: Do you solemnly (swear/affirm) that this statement is true, (so help you God / on your honor)?

Signer 1 Name and Address:			Signer 2 Name and Address:		

Identification Method: ☐ Personally Known ☐ Other
☐ Texas Driver's License ☐ Driver's License ☐ Passport

Identification Method: ☐ Personally Known ☐ Other
☐ Texas Driver's License ☐ Driver's License ☐ Passport

Sign Here

X _____

Sign Here

X _____

Date/Time: Ref#:

Signing Address:

Document Date	Notarization **A**ck **J**ur **O**th Fee if any	Document Description	Signer Initials	
			1	2
		Deed of Trust / Mortgage		
		Deed - General - Quit Claim - Special Warranty		
		Borrower's Title Affidavit		
		Borrower's Closing Affidavit		
		E&O / Compliance Agreement		
		Occupancy Affidavit		
		Signature Name Affidavit		
		Power of Attorney - Limited / Durable		
		T-47 Residential Real Property Affidavit		
		Mineral Rights Acknowledgement and Agreement		
		Designation of Homestead / Non-Homestead		
		Notice of Penalties for Making False or Misleading Statements		
		Ownership Affidavit		
		Occupancy and Financial Status Affidavit		
		Obligation of Debts Affidavit		
		Release of Claims and Hold Harmless Agreement		
		Affidavit of Marital Status		
		Tax Indemnity		
		Compliance / Correction Agreement		

Notes:

Ack:Do you acknowledge this as your signature and your free act and deed, for the purposes stated herein?
Jurat: Do you solemnly (swear/affirm) that this statement is true, (so help you God / on your honor)?

Signer 1 Name and Address:		Signer 2 Name and Address:	

Identification Method: ☐ Personally Known ☐ Other ☐ Texas Driver's License ☐ Driver's License ☐ Passport	Identification Method: ☐ Personally Known ☐ Other ☐ Texas Driver's License ☐ Driver's License ☐ Passport

Sign Here

Sign Here

X _____ X _____

Date/Time:	Ref#:

Signing Address:

Document Date	Notarization **A**ck **J**ur **O**th Fee if any	Document Description	Signer Initials	
			1	2
		Deed of Trust / Mortgage		
		Deed - General - Quit Claim - Special Warranty		
		Borrower's Title Affidavit		
		Borrower's Closing Affidavit		
		E&O / Compliance Agreement		
		Occupancy Affidavit		
		Signature Name Affidavit		
		Power of Attorney - Limited / Durable		
		T-47 Residential Real Property Affidavit		
		Mineral Rights Acknowledgement and Agreement		
		Designation of Homestead / Non-Homestead		
		Notice of Penalties for Making False or Misleading Statements		
		Ownership Affidavit		
		Occupancy and Financial Status Affidavit		
		Obligation of Debts Affidavit		
		Release of Claims and Hold Harmless Agreement		
		Affidavit of Marital Status		
		Tax Indemnity		
		Compliance / Correction Agreement		

Notes:

Ack: Do you acknowledge this as your signature and your free act and deed, for the purposes stated herein?
Jurat: Do you solemnly (swear/affirm) that this statement is true, (so help you God / on your honor)?

| Signer 1 Name and Address: | | Signer 2 Name and Address: | |

Identification Method:☐ Personally Known ☐ Other
☐ Texas Driver's License ☐ Driver's License ☐ Passport

Identification Method:☐ Personally Known ☐ Other
☐ Texas Driver's License ☐ Driver's License ☐ Passport

Sign Here   Sign Here

X _____   X _____

Date/Time: Ref#:

Signing Address:

Document Date	Notarization **A**ck Jur **O**th Fee if any	Document Description	Signer Initials	
			1	2
		Deed of Trust / Mortgage		
		Deed - General - Quit Claim - Special Warranty		
		Borrower's Title Affidavit		
		Borrower's Closing Affidavit		
		E&O / Compliance Agreement		
		Occupancy Affidavit		
		Signature Name Affidavit		
		Power of Attorney - Limited / Durable		
		T-47 Residential Real Property Affidavit		
		Mineral Rights Acknowledgement and Agreement		
		Designation of Homestead / Non-Homestead		
		Notice of Penalties for Making False or Misleading Statements		
		Ownership Affidavit		
		Occupancy and Financial Status Affidavit		
		Obligation of Debts Affidavit		
		Release of Claims and Hold Harmless Agreement		
		Affidavit of Marital Status		
		Tax Indemnity		
		Compliance / Correction Agreement		

Notes:

Ack:Do you acknowledge this as your signature and your free act and deed, for the purposes stated herein?
Jurat: Do you solemnly (swear/affirm) that this statement is true, (so help you God / on your honor)?

Signer 1 Name and Address:		Signer 2 Name and Address:	
Identification Method:☐ Personally Known ☐ Other ☐ Texas Driver's License ☐ Driver's License ☐ Passport		Identification Method:☐ Personally Known ☐ Other ☐ Texas Driver's License ☐ Driver's License ☐ Passport	
X _____		X _____	
Date/Time:		Ref#:	
Signing Address:			

Document Date	Notarization **A**ck **J**ur **O**th Fee if any	Document Description	Signer Initials	
			1	2
		Deed of Trust / Mortgage		
		Deed - General - Quit Claim - Special Warranty		
		Borrower's Title Affidavit		
		Borrower's Closing Affidavit		
		E&O / Compliance Agreement		
		Occupancy Affidavit		
		Signature Name Affidavit		
		Power of Attorney - Limited / Durable		
		T-47 Residential Real Property Affidavit		
		Mineral Rights Acknowledgement and Agreement		
		Designation of Homestead / Non-Homestead		
		Notice of Penalties for Making False or Misleading Statements		
		Ownership Affidavit		
		Occupancy and Financial Status Affidavit		
		Obligation of Debts Affidavit		
		Release of Claims and Hold Harmless Agreement		
		Affidavit of Marital Status		
		Tax Indemnity		
		Compliance / Correction Agreement		

Notes:

Ack:Do you acknowledge this as your signature and your free act and deed, for the purposes stated herein?
Jurat: Do you solemnly (swear/affirm) that this statement is true, (so help you God / on your honor)?

Signer 1 Name and Address:		Signer 2 Name and Address:	
Identification Method: ☐ Personally Known ☐ Other ☐ Texas Driver's License ☐ Driver's License ☐ Passport		Identification Method: ☐ Personally Known ☐ Other ☐ Texas Driver's License ☐ Driver's License ☐ Passport	
Sign Here X _____		Sign Here X _____	

Date/Time: Ref#:

Signing Address:

Document Date	Notarization **A**ck **J**ur **O**th Fee if any	Document Description	Signer Initials	
			1	2
		Deed of Trust / Mortgage		
		Deed - General - Quit Claim - Special Warranty		
		Borrower's Title Affidavit		
		Borrower's Closing Affidavit		
		E&O / Compliance Agreement		
		Occupancy Affidavit		
		Signature Name Affidavit		
		Power of Attorney - Limited / Durable		
		T-47 Residential Real Property Affidavit		
		Mineral Rights Acknowledgement and Agreement		
		Designation of Homestead / Non-Homestead		
		Notice of Penalties for Making False or Misleading Statements		
		Ownership Affidavit		
		Occupancy and Financial Status Affidavit		
		Obligation of Debts Affidavit		
		Release of Claims and Hold Harmless Agreement		
		Affidavit of Marital Status		
		Tax Indemnity		
		Compliance / Correction Agreement		

Notes:

Ack: Do you acknowledge this as your signature and your free act and deed, for the purposes stated herein?
Jurat: Do you solemnly (swear/affirm) that this statement is true, (so help you God / on your honor)?

89

Signer 1 Name and Address:		Signer 2 Name and Address:	
Identification Method:☐ Personally Known ☐ Other ☐ Texas Driver's License ☐ Driver's License ☐ Passport		Identification Method:☐ Personally Known ☐ Other ☐ Texas Driver's License ☐ Driver's License ☐ Passport	
Sign Here X _____		Sign Here X _____	
Date/Time:		Ref#:	
Signing Address:			

Document Date	Notarization **A**ck **J**ur **O**th Fee if any	Document Description	Signer Initials	
			1	2
		Deed of Trust / Mortgage		
		Deed - General - Quit Claim - Special Warranty		
		Borrower's Title Affidavit		
		Borrower's Closing Affidavit		
		E&O / Compliance Agreement		
		Occupancy Affidavit		
		Signature Name Affidavit		
		Power of Attorney - Limited / Durable		
		T-47 Residential Real Property Affidavit		
		Mineral Rights Acknowledgement and Agreement		
		Designation of Homestead / Non-Homestead		
		Notice of Penalties for Making False or Misleading Statements		
		Ownership Affidavit		
		Occupancy and Financial Status Affidavit		
		Obligation of Debts Affidavit		
		Release of Claims and Hold Harmless Agreement		
		Affidavit of Marital Status		
		Tax Indemnity		
		Compliance / Correction Agreement		

Notes:			

Ack:Do you acknowledge this as your signature and your free act and deed, for the purposes stated herein?
Jurat: Do you solemnly (swear/affirm) that this statement is true, (so help you God / on your honor)?

| Signer 1 Name and Address: | | Signer 2 Name and Address: | |

| Identification Method:☐ Personally Known ☐ Other | Identification Method:☐ Personally Known ☐ Other |
| ☐ Texas Driver's License ☐ Driver's License ☐ Passport | ☐ Texas Driver's License ☐ Driver's License ☐ Passport |

Sign Here

X _____

Sign Here

X _____

Date/Time: Ref#:

Signing Address:

Document Date	Notarization **A**ck **J**ur **O**th Fee if any	Document Description	Signer Initials	
			1	2
		Deed of Trust / Mortgage		
		Deed - General - Quit Claim - Special Warranty		
		Borrower's Title Affidavit		
		Borrower's Closing Affidavit		
		E&O / Compliance Agreement		
		Occupancy Affidavit		
		Signature Name Affidavit		
		Power of Attorney - Limited / Durable		
		T-47 Residential Real Property Affidavit		
		Mineral Rights Acknowledgement and Agreement		
		Designation of Homestead / Non-Homestead		
		Notice of Penalties for Making False or Misleading Statements		
		Ownership Affidavit		
		Occupancy and Financial Status Affidavit		
		Obligation of Debts Affidavit		
		Release of Claims and Hold Harmless Agreement		
		Affidavit of Marital Status		
		Tax Indemnity		
		Compliance / Correction Agreement		

Notes:

Ack:Do you acknowledge this as your signature and your free act and deed, for the purposes stated herein?
Jurat: Do you solemnly (swear/affirm) that this statement is true, (so help you God / on your honor)?

Signer 1 Name and Address:		Signer 2 Name and Address:	
Identification Method:☐ Personally Known ☐ Other ☐ Texas Driver's License ☐ Driver's License ☐ Passport		Identification Method:☐ Personally Known ☐ Other ☐ Texas Driver's License ☐ Driver's License ☐ Passport	
X _____		X _____	
Date/Time:		Ref#:	

Signing Address:

Document Date	Notarization **A**ck **J**ur **O**th Fee if any	Document Description	Signer Initials	
			1	2
		Deed of Trust / Mortgage		
		Deed - General - Quit Claim - Special Warranty		
		Borrower's Title Affidavit		
		Borrower's Closing Affidavit		
		E&O / Compliance Agreement		
		Occupancy Affidavit		
		Signature Name Affidavit		
		Power of Attorney - Limited / Durable		
		T-47 Residential Real Property Affidavit		
		Mineral Rights Acknowledgement and Agreement		
		Designation of Homestead / Non-Homestead		
		Notice of Penalties for Making False or Misleading Statements		
		Ownership Affidavit		
		Occupancy and Financial Status Affidavit		
		Obligation of Debts Affidavit		
		Release of Claims and Hold Harmless Agreement		
		Affidavit of Marital Status		
		Tax Indemnity		
		Compliance / Correction Agreement		

Notes:

Ack: Do you acknowledge this as your signature and your free act and deed, for the purposes stated herein?
Jurat: Do you solemnly (swear/affirm) that this statement is true, (so help you God / on your honor)?
92

Signer 1 Name and Address:		Signer 2 Name and Address:		

Identification Method:☐ Personally Known ☐ Other
☐ Texas Driver's License ☐ Driver's License ☐ Passport

Identification Method:☐ Personally Known ☐ Other
☐ Texas Driver's License ☐ Driver's License ☐ Passport

Sign Here

Sign Here

X _____

X _____

Date/Time:

Ref#:

Signing Address:

Document Date	Notarization **A**ck **J**ur **O**th Fee if any	Document Description	Signer Initials	
			1	2
		Deed of Trust / Mortgage		
		Deed - General - Quit Claim - Special Warranty		
		Borrower's Title Affidavit		
		Borrower's Closing Affidavit		
		E&O / Compliance Agreement		
		Occupancy Affidavit		
		Signature Name Affidavit		
		Power of Attorney - Limited / Durable		
		T-47 Residential Real Property Affidavit		
		Mineral Rights Acknowledgement and Agreement		
		Designation of Homestead / Non-Homestead		
		Notice of Penalties for Making False or Misleading Statements		
		Ownership Affidavit		
		Occupancy and Financial Status Affidavit		
		Obligation of Debts Affidavit		
		Release of Claims and Hold Harmless Agreement		
		Affidavit of Marital Status		
		Tax Indemnity		
		Compliance / Correction Agreement		

Notes:

Ack:Do you acknowledge this as your signature and your free act and deed, for the purposes stated herein?
Jurat: Do you solemnly (swear/affirm) that this statement is true, (so help you God / on your honor)?

| Signer 1 Name and Address: | | Signer 2 Name and Address: | |

| Identification Method:☐ Personally Known   ☐ Other | | Identification Method:☐ Personally Known   ☐ Other | |
| ☐ Texas Driver's License ☐ Driver's License ☐ Passport | | ☐ Texas Driver's License ☐ Driver's License ☐ Passport | |

Sign Here   Sign Here

X _____   X _____

Date/Time: **Ref#:**

Signing Address:

Document Date	Notarization **A**ck **J**ur **O**th Fee if any	Document Description	Signer Initials	
			1	2
		Deed of Trust / Mortgage		
		Deed - General - Quit Claim - Special Warranty		
		Borrower's Title Affidavit		
		Borrower's Closing Affidavit		
		E&O / Compliance Agreement		
		Occupancy Affidavit		
		Signature Name Affidavit		
		Power of Attorney - Limited / Durable		
		T-47 Residential Real Property Affidavit		
		Mineral Rights Acknowledgement and Agreement		
		Designation of Homestead / Non-Homestead		
		Notice of Penalties for Making False or Misleading Statements		
		Ownership Affidavit		
		Occupancy and Financial Status Affidavit		
		Obligation of Debts Affidavit		
		Release of Claims and Hold Harmless Agreement		
		Affidavit of Marital Status		
		Tax Indemnity		
		Compliance / Correction Agreement		

Notes:

Ack:Do you acknowledge this as your signature and your free act and deed, for the purposes stated herein?
Jurat: Do you solemnly (swear/affirm) that this statement is true, (so help you God / on your honor)?

Signer 1 Name and Address:			Signer 2 Name and Address:		

Identification Method: ☐ Personally Known   ☐ Other
☐ Texas Driver's License ☐ Driver's License ☐ Passport

Identification Method: ☐ Personally Known   ☐ Other
☐ Texas Driver's License ☐ Driver's License ☐ Passport

Sign Here

Sign Here

X _____

X _____

Date/Time: **Ref#:**

Signing Address:

Document Date	Notarization **A**ck **J**ur **O**th Fee if any	Document Description	Signer Initials	
			1	2
		Deed of Trust / Mortgage		
		Deed - General - Quit Claim - Special Warranty		
		Borrower's Title Affidavit		
		Borrower's Closing Affidavit		
		E&O / Compliance Agreement		
		Occupancy Affidavit		
		Signature Name Affidavit		
		Power of Attorney - Limited / Durable		
		T-47 Residential Real Property Affidavit		
		Mineral Rights Acknowledgement and Agreement		
		Designation of Homestead / Non-Homestead		
		Notice of Penalties for Making False or Misleading Statements		
		Ownership Affidavit		
		Occupancy and Financial Status Affidavit		
		Obligation of Debts Affidavit		
		Release of Claims and Hold Harmless Agreement		
		Affidavit of Marital Status		
		Tax Indemnity		
		Compliance / Correction Agreement		

Notes:

Ack:Do you acknowledge this as your signature and your free act and deed, for the purposes stated herein?
Jurat: Do you solemnly (swear/affirm) that this statement is true, (so help you God / on your honor)?

Signer 1 Name and Address:		Signer 2 Name and Address:	

Identification Method:☐ Personally Known ☐ Other ☐ Texas Driver's License ☐ Driver's License ☐ Passport		Identification Method:☐ Personally Known ☐ Other ☐ Texas Driver's License ☐ Driver's License ☐ Passport	

Sign Here

Sign Here

X _____   X _____

Date/Time:	Ref#:

Signing Address:

Document Date	Notarization **A**ck **J**ur **O**th Fee if any	Document Description	Signer Initials	
			1	2
		Deed of Trust / Mortgage		
		Deed - General - Quit Claim - Special Warranty		
		Borrower's Title Affidavit		
		Borrower's Closing Affidavit		
		E&O / Compliance Agreement		
		Occupancy Affidavit		
		Signature Name Affidavit		
		Power of Attorney - Limited / Durable		
		T-47 Residential Real Property Affidavit		
		Mineral Rights Acknowledgement and Agreement		
		Designation of Homestead / Non-Homestead		
		Notice of Penalties for Making False or Misleading Statements		
		Ownership Affidavit		
		Occupancy and Financial Status Affidavit		
		Obligation of Debts Affidavit		
		Release of Claims and Hold Harmless Agreement		
		Affidavit of Marital Status		
		Tax Indemnity		
		Compliance / Correction Agreement		

Notes:

Ack:Do you acknowledge this as your signature and your free act and deed, for the purposes stated herein?
Jurat: Do you solemnly (swear/affirm) that this statement is true, (so help you God / on your honor)?

Signer 1 Name and Address:		Signer 2 Name and Address:	
Identification Method:☐ Personally Known ☐ Other ☐ Texas Driver's License ☐ Driver's License ☐ Passport		Identification Method:☐ Personally Known ☐ Other ☐ Texas Driver's License ☐ Driver's License ☐ Passport	

Sign Here   Sign Here

X _____   X _____

Date/Time: Ref#:

Signing Address:

Document Date	Notarization **A**ck **J**ur **O**th Fee if any	Document Description	Signer Initials	
			1	2
		Deed of Trust / Mortgage		
		Deed - General - Quit Claim - Special Warranty		
		Borrower's Title Affidavit		
		Borrower's Closing Affidavit		
		E&O / Compliance Agreement		
		Occupancy Affidavit		
		Signature Name Affidavit		
		Power of Attorney - Limited / Durable		
		T-47 Residential Real Property Affidavit		
		Mineral Rights Acknowledgement and Agreement		
		Designation of Homestead / Non-Homestead		
		Notice of Penalties for Making False or Misleading Statements		
		Ownership Affidavit		
		Occupancy and Financial Status Affidavit		
		Obligation of Debts Affidavit		
		Release of Claims and Hold Harmless Agreement		
		Affidavit of Marital Status		
		Tax Indemnity		
		Compliance / Correction Agreement		

Notes:

Ack:Do you acknowledge this as your signature and your free act and deed, for the purposes stated herein?
Jurat: Do you solemnly (swear/affirm) that this statement is true, (so help you God / on your honor)?

Signer 1 Name and Address:		Signer 2 Name and Address:	

Identification Method:☐ Personally Known ☐ Other
☐ Texas Driver's License ☐ Driver's License ☐ Passport

Identification Method:☐ Personally Known ☐ Other
☐ Texas Driver's License ☐ Driver's License ☐ Passport

Sign Here

X _____

Sign Here

X _____

Date/Time: Ref#:

Signing Address:

Document Date	Notarization **A**ck **J**ur **O**th Fee if any	Document Description	Signer Initials	
			1	2
		Deed of Trust / Mortgage		
		Deed - General - Quit Claim - Special Warranty		
		Borrower's Title Affidavit		
		Borrower's Closing Affidavit		
		E&O / Compliance Agreement		
		Occupancy Affidavit		
		Signature Name Affidavit		
		Power of Attorney - Limited / Durable		
		T-47 Residential Real Property Affidavit		
		Mineral Rights Acknowledgement and Agreement		
		Designation of Homestead / Non-Homestead		
		Notice of Penalties for Making False or Misleading Statements		
		Ownership Affidavit		
		Occupancy and Financial Status Affidavit		
		Obligation of Debts Affidavit		
		Release of Claims and Hold Harmless Agreement		
		Affidavit of Marital Status		
		Tax Indemnity		
		Compliance / Correction Agreement		

Notes:

Ack:Do you acknowledge this as your signature and your free act and deed, for the purposes stated herein?
Jurat: Do you solemnly (swear/affirm) that this statement is true, (so help you God / on your honor)?